Writing: MAN'S GREAT INVENTION

A Publication of the Peabody Institute

THE CRADLE OF OUR CIVILIZATION

Scale 0 — 300 Miles

SEA
Phasis
COLCHIS
Trapezus
PONTUS
Armavir
Artaxata
Ararat
ARMENIA
CASPIAN SEA
L. Van
Amida
MESOPOTAMIA
Carchemish
Thapsacus
Euphrates R.
Nineveh
Arbela
ASSYRIA
Ashur
Tigris
MEDIA
Raghæ
Ecbatana
Palmyra
Tingat
Kit
Kes Upi
SYRIAN DESERT
ELAM
Babylon
Kish
AKKAD
SUMER
Lagash
Susa
Erech
Ur
Eridu
PERSIS
present shore
Persepolis
ARABIAN
PERSIAN GULF
DESERT
Gerrha
Raise

MAN'S GREAT INVENTION

by J. Hambleton Ober

Baltimore, Maryland

Gratefully dedicated to my wife without whose patience and encouragement this book would not have been written.

Books on writing fall into two kinds, those written by scholars and those written by laymen. The former have the authority of their learned authors but are usually beyond the understanding of readers with little academic training. The latter, while simple and readable, often contain errors in content. Mr. Ober conceived the plan of this book so as to have both scholarly authority and readableness. He himself, posing as the layman, laid out the general plan and wrote the first draft. Then he submitted it to scholars of Johns Hopkins University, who went over the sections on which they are specialists and subjected the factual content to a severe scrutiny. The following pages have resulted from this consultation between the author and the authorities.

The following are members of the Johns Hopkins faculty who have cooperated: George F. Carter for symbols and pictographs; W. G. Lambert for cuneiform and

Preface

Semitic scripts; James W. Poultney for the Greek and Latin alphabets and Cretan writing; and Hans Goedicke for ancient Egyptian writing. Every field of scholarly work has its problems, and our attitude has been to present what is the generally accepted opinion of those competent to judge, and not to concern ourselves with unproven theories or doubtful opinions. It will be understood that many things in the ancient world cannot be dated exactly. In such cases we have given approximate figures.

We are satisfied that this book supplies a big need, for we know of no other book in English that presents both a readable and yet a thoroughly reliable account of one of the great achievements of civilized man—writing.

W. G. LAMBERT
Chairman of the Oriental Seminary
of Johns Hopkins University
May, 1964

Table of Contents

List of Illustrations, Charts & Maps

LETTER CHARTS

MAPS

Often when I have been reading, the self-evident thought has occurred to me that the book—any book—I was reading could not have been written until man had learned the art of writing; that I, like many others, took writing as much for granted as the air we breathe. And yet, although writing is one of the greatest achievements of civilized man, its history is not taught in school or college. True, there are many technical volumes for scholars to study but, to my surprise, I found that very little had been written for a layman, such as myself, who wants the story told simply and made clear with maps, charts and illustrations.

I decided to undertake that task. That it was a bold undertaking became obvious from the start. I would need aid from many sources. Therefore I made this book a project of the Peabody Institute of which I have been a trustee for many years. In the 1880s and '90s, its

Introduction

xiii

library had served the newly founded Johns Hopkins University. It is one of the best known libraries in the country.

The main purpose of this book is to tell the story of our own alphabet, the history of which can be traced back through successive stages of development to a primitive stage when all records were merely the pictures of things or words or ideas. It is not the purpose of this book to relate the history of all systems of writing. Therefore, the reader will find a reference only now and then to the Chinese and Japanese, to the Hindus and Mayans and others.

Although cuneiform probably was not in the direct line of ancestry of the English alphabet, any book on writing would be incomplete without an account of cuneiform, which is one of the oldest and most important systems of writing.

For no reason other than that interest in Crete has been quickened by the decipherment of Linear B by Michael Ventris and John Chadwick in 1953, I have included a short chapter on Crete and Linear B. W. F. Albright considers this brilliant feat to be the most striking advance in decipherment. Chronologically this chapter should come after the chapter on Egypt. However, the line of ancestry of our alphabet does not directly include the Cretan scripts; thus the chapter on "The Cretans" has been placed earlier in this book.

Frank N. Jones, Director of Peabody Library; P. W. Filby, Assistant Director; Alice Meyers, the library staff, and others have lent a helping hand, directly or indirectly, knowingly or unknowingly. For their help and support I tender my sincere gratitude.

Expert aid was given without stint by George F. Carter, Hans Goedicke, W. G. Lambert, and James W. Poultney of the Johns Hopkins University and also A. Sachs of Brown University. All corrections and revisions, as suggested by them, have been carried out. For their time and generous cooperation I am deeply grateful. They kept the author from stumbling into many errors but are not responsible for whatever deficiencies may have been caused by the author's literary idiosyncrasies, nor for the fact that here and there I have put in something for no better reason than that it interested me.

The author and the publishers are grateful for permission to include in this book illustrations and other material from the sources listed under Acknowledgments.

Acknowledgements

British Museum; Antichita dell'Etruria, Florence, Italy; Museo Archeologico, Florence, Italy; National Museum of Damascus; The Historical Society of Pennsylvania; American Museum of Natural History; Oriental Institute, University of Chicago; Metropolitan Museum of Art, New York; The Johns Hopkins Press; *Art of The World—The Stone Age,* edited by Hans-Georg Bandi, used by permission of Crown Publishers, Inc.; *The Ogham Inscribed Monuments of Gaedhl* by G. R. Brash; David Diringer from his books on *Writing* and *The Alphabet*; *They Wrote on Clay* by Edward Chiera, by permission of University of Chicago Press; *The Romance of Writing,* written and illustrated by Keith Gordon Irwin, by permission of The Viking Press; *Voices in Stone* by Ernst Doblhofer, by permission of The Viking Press; *Die Schrift* by H. D. Jensen; *Die kretische Schrift entziffert* by W. Merlinger; *Rock Pictures of Europe* by

Herbert Kühn; *Archaeology of Palestine* by William F. Albright; *Linguistic Science in the Nineteenth Century* by Holger Pedersen, by permission of Harvard University Press; *The Decipherment of Linear B* by John Chadwick, by permission of Cambridge University Press; *The Triumph of The Alphabet* by Alfred C. Moorhouse, by permission of Abelard-Schuman Limited; *The Secret of the Peruvian Quipus* by Erland Nordenskiöld.

To Hans Goedicke, W. G. Lambert and James W. Poultney of Johns Hopkins University for preparing the charts of letter signs and a number of the illustrations in Chapters V, VII, and VIII.

To Ruth Bornschlegel and P. W. Filby for other illustrations throughout the book.

To Dr. Erwin Raisz for preparation of the maps. Dr. Raisz was with Harvard's Institute of Geographical Exploration for twenty years and is the author of specialized texts, atlases and other works. He has drawn maps to illustrate books by Samuel Eliot Morison, Bernard DeVoto and others.

Writing: MAN'S GREAT INVENTION

Courtesy of the American Museum of Natural History
Artists in the cave of Fort de Gaume, France (Mural by Charles R. Knight)

How Writing Developed

In this twentieth century we take the letters of our alphabet as much for granted as the air we breathe. We learn to write at such an early age that we seldom stop to think about the importance of writing to mankind. How many of us realize that writing alone has made possible the greatest civilizations and cultures, the great empires of the human race? Abraham Lincoln once said that writing has enabled us to "converse with the dead, the absent, the unborn, at all distances of time and space."

There never was a first man who could sit down and say, "Now I am going to write." That supreme achievement of man was the result of a slow and natural development over thousands of years. What did the first attempt at writing look like? Was it printed or written by hand? Where can it be found?

Some say that writing begins with cave paintings, which throw light on the distant past in various parts of the world. They argue that every one of our letters was originally a picture of some object.

Curiously enough, the very word "alphabet" betrays its pictorial origin, for it is nothing more than a combination of the names of the first two letters in the ancient Greek alphabet, *alpha* and *beta,* which came from the Semitic letters *'āleph* and *bēth. 'Āleph* means ox. This letter, which ultimately developed into our *a,* was at first a drawing of the head of an ox. *Bēth* is Semitic for house; the original *b* was a drawing of a house.

Many have proved to their satisfaction that writing began with cuneiform, while others have argued that hieroglyphics have a prior claim. So one thing becomes very clear at the outset. There is no generally accepted birth certificate, as it were, for our alphabet. If there were, our story would be simple, but not nearly so interesting.

Although difference of opinion seems to be the air scholars breathe, they do find easy agreement in the fact that civilization did not develop in the same way and at the same time among all peoples throughout the world. Five thousand years ago the Egyptians could boast of a great civilization. Today, the Bushmen of Africa still lead the most primitive of lives.

The same is true of writing. It did not evolve

in the same way and at the same time among all peoples. The Greeks were using a fully developed alphabet over twenty-five hundred years ago. Today, many peoples have nothing better than a primitive system of writing. In quite recent times the Eskimos, the Hottentots and other peoples were using picture-writing and it is generally accepted that all writing systems started with pictures.

With the following basic chart as a guide, the part played by each stage of writing and by the scripts of many peoples will be more easily understood as we get along into the history of writing.

STAGES IN THE DEVELOPMENT OF WRITING

PRELIMINARY—DEVICES FOR COMMUNICATION

Memory Aids   Symbolic Devices   Storytellers

PICTURE-WRITING

Pictographs   Ideograms

PHONETIC OR SOUND-WRITING

Syllabaries
Semitic Consonant Alphabet
Greek Complete Alphabet

Just a casual glance shows that there were two distinct and different ways of writing, one using pictures, the other using syllables or letters to express sounds. But do not be misled into thinking that ancient picture-writing was dropped when sound-writing began, for we make use of pictures along with our alphabet today. We also find good use for the devices employed by man for communication before he learned to write, some being easier, quicker and surer methods of communication than our own written language.

Transition between the stages in the development of writing was gradual. One stage was not abandoned when the next began. They were intermingled: They did not follow in a line but were piled upon one another. This means that we find picture-writing and sound-writing coexisting in the same system. Indeed, the greatest of the ancient systems that have died out, Egyptian hieroglyphics and Babylonian cuneiform, always kept both kinds of writing in use together. It is only in the alphabetic system that picture-writing has for the most part become extinct, its chief survival being in numerals.

Today, man records the present by means of his writing, his pictures and photographs. Prehistoric man did the same through his pictures and carvings, which speak to people in any language after many millenia. Along with other finds made by the archeologists, they give us a rich, realistic and colorful insight into the ways of life of our remote ancestors, their religions, their material culture and history.

Picture-writings are found everywhere, for primitive people everywhere discovered that events could be recorded and messages conveyed by means of pictures. In picture-writing we have the first step in the development of all writing.

Many contend that primitive man's pictures belong to the history of art, or of very ancient religious beliefs or of most venerable hunting magic, and no doubt some were just that. But many more were doubtless narrative and told a story to the people of that time. We find successful hunting expeditions portrayed and important battles recorded for the benefit of contemporaries or, possibly, posterity.

The fact that hunting involved danger is told in this picture of a wounded wild ox pursuing a hunter.

Hunter pursued by wild ox *

The kind of weapons used is indicated by the picture of a bison with arrow and boomerangs.

Bison with arrow and boomerangs

Even the means of transportation or sport is shown in a rock engraving from Norway of a man on snowshoes or skis.

*From THE ART OF THE STONE AGE *edited by Hans-Georg Bandi.* *Used by permission of Crown Publishers, Inc.*

The early primitive artist made his pictures as beautiful and accurate as possible. If he made a picture of a gazelle, it was not writing but simply a work of art. If he discovered the presence of gazelles in a certain place and drew a picture of them to tell his friends that it was a good hunting ground, then his picture was no longer a work of art, it was a message. That one picture says: "Here are gazelles." He might make a picture of a lion with gazelles. Primitive man would have no difficulty in reading the warning: "Good hunting but watch out."

Then man discovered that he could tell just as much with far less trouble. So he left many details out of his lifelike pictures and drew only silhouettes of the figures of men and animals, sometimes only the head of an animal.

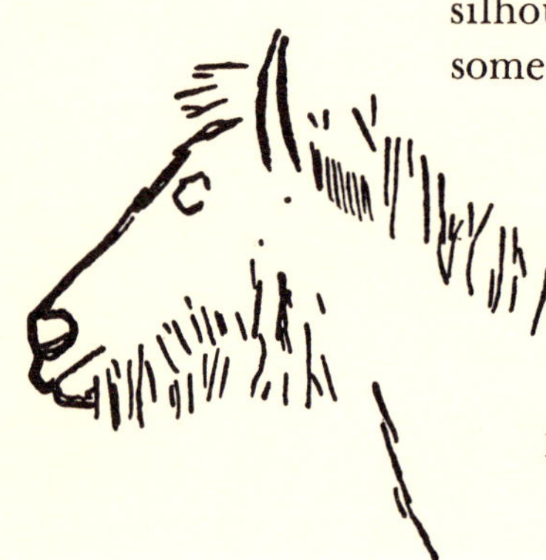

Head of a wild horse

In a later stage the figures became so simplified that they were merely stylized or conventional figures. Thus the picture of a man was reduced to a simple sign. Another step in writing had been made.

man

But all this did not spring up overnight. As time went on, one man may have scratched his head and said to another, "If I add a spear to my

man sign, the sign will show the man is a warrior." Nodding to himself, he quickly drew his
new sign. Or some other artist may have added
arrows for a hunter or warrior.

It was easy to represent concrete things. If one
wished to indicate an animal or a man, he simply
drew a picture. (These pictures, conventionalized
symbols of beasts, man or things, are called *pictographs.*) But the picture could not express an
abstract idea. The drawer could not make the people in his pictures speak, as it were. If he were
going to show their thoughts and feelings, he
needed a brand new kind of picture. The picture
of an eye with tears dropping from it is to be
seen not only in a crude California rock drawing but also in the more highly developed
Maya and Aztec scripts as well as in the early
hieroglyphic and Chinese writings.

That single picture means to sorrow or weep,
without words in any language. Man had grasped
the advantage of associating certain pictographs
with certain ideas. So from his pictographs man
gradually evolved the use of what we call *ideograms,* which represent not so much the thing they
show as the underlying idea associated with the
thing. For example, an ear does not only indicate
a part of human anatomy, it also gives the idea of
hearing. Man had learned to draw idea-pictures as
well as thing-pictures and he used them both to
write better than ever before. He had made the
second step in the art of writing.

Man has never abandoned his picture-writing.
For instance, we use the pointing hand and many
other examples today. However, as the centuries

went by and civilization grew more complex, man found that his picture writing was not adequate for all his needs. Thus he advanced to the further step where the pictures, or the characters derived from them, suggested a sound rather than an object or an idea. Signs of this kind, which represent sounds, are called *phonograms* and writing systems which employ them are called *phonetic.*

Between picture-writing and phonetic writing, where the sign for a sound is bound up with the language, there is a big gap. Still it should not be too difficult to reconstruct the first step in the advance toward phonetic writing.

Picture-writing, as we have seen, arose independently of language. Pictorial and ideographic signs can be understood without reference to  words. For example, the man sign represents a human being, but the word for human being is different in every language.

In early picture-writing, for all of the things for which there were signs, there were also words, but between the words and the signs there was originally no link at all. That link was forged when man finally recognized that a picture not only conveys an image but also a word that is used for the depicted object. Thus in time it was realized that a pictograph could stand not only for the object but also for the sound when the word for the object was spoken. This being so, it was possible to attach to a pictograph or sign a phonetic value independent of the meaning which it had as a word. Thus a drawing of a tree and a pan would express the word *trepan.*

Sound-writing, however, went through more

than one step before the complete alphabet came into being. The next step toward sound-writing was the development of a syllabary, when man learned that words were capable of being divided into syllables. A syllabic system of writing seems to have come more easily to some people than that of an alphabet.

To the Babylonians, Cretans and others there was nothing peculiar about a syllabic system of writing. Indeed, they had every right to be proud of it. It was an enormous advance over picture-writing and served their needs quite well.

As we know, a syllable is only a vowel sound or the combination of a vowel and one or more consonants. Therefore in a syllabary each syllable is represented by a single sign and the words are written by stringing out a number of syllables. In other words, a syllabic system splits up words like a child's first reading book; thus "in-di-vi-du-al" requires five signs; "fa-mi-ly," only three.

Could anything be simpler? Then why do we need an alphabet? Well, imagine writing the word "strength," which is one syllable, with a single sign. This example shows how clumsy a syllabic system of writing can be when a language uses complicated groups of consonants. True, the total number of signs in a syllabic system is less than the number required in a pictographic system, but it is still much higher than the number required in an alphabet and can be uneconomical.

Instead of our twenty-six letters, hundreds of signs were needed by the Babylonians for the purpose of combining syllables into words. Thus there had to be a separate written sign for each of the

syllables *ba, be, bi, bu, ab, eb, ib, ub,* and so on. The Babylonians used 350 signs. Their sign for *ba* and *pa* are shown here.

From the practical standpoint alone a syllabic system of writing would be hopeless for us. Try to invent a typewriter for the number of signs required for a syllabary. The Japanese are plagued with that problem.

So now we come to alphabetic writing, which we may fairly regard as the finished product of this long train of development. By now it must be obvious that a complete alphabet is the highest form of writing—in part, because of the smaller number of signs needed for letters in comparison to the number required for picture-writing, or a syllabary; in part, because the essence of an alphabet is that each alphabetic sign stands for a single vowel or consonant.

And here two steps seem to have been taken before the complete alphabet of the Greeks came into being. The alphabet, which the Greeks borrowed from the Semites, was made up of signs for consonants alone. There were no signs for vowels, so the reader had to supply the vowel which suited the context.

We have shown the Semitic system of writing as a consonant alphabet; however, some scholars hold that the Semitic writing was not alphabetic. Strictly speaking, they say, we should treat the Semitic script as syllabic, not as alphabetic. However, the distinguished linguist Holger Pedersen lists the Semitic script under the alphabetical systems with the notation, "The Semitic alphabet, a syllabic script, which to us may seem to be a consonant-script."

It should not be surprising, then, that other scholars hold the Semitic system to be an alphabet for consonant writing and that they refer to the Semites as inventors of the alphabet. Nor should it be unreasonable if we treat the Semitic script as a consonant alphabet, because it is not intended in this book to deal broadly with technical details of controversial theories.

It has been stated that the Greeks borrowed the Semitic consonantal alphabet, so right here seems to be the place for a few words about languages and pronunciation, about consonants and vowels, and about borrowed alphabets.

It is a curious fact that people often forget that an alphabet or a system of writing is altogether distinct from the speech which it is used to represent. Nowadays the same script can be used for various languages. Such is the case of the Latin alphabet, which is employed for English, French, German, and so on. In ancient times the Semitic-speaking Babylonians used the cuneiform writing which they took over from the non-Semitic Sumerians.

Likewise, the same speech can be expressed in different scripts. For instance, the Arabic spoken in North Africa is written in the Arabic alphabet, but the Arabic spoken in Malta is written in the Latin alphabet.

Therefore, in the story of writing much is told about languages; about languages and writing systems not always being the same; about one people borrowing a system of writing from another people and adapting it to their own language. The best known example of this is the way the Greeks borrowed the Phoenician-Semitic alphabet and adapted it to their own language.

It seems an impossible task to read and understand something written only in consonants. When we abbreviate "boulevard" to "blvd.," this abbreviation is made up entirely of consonants. Although there are no vowels, we are so accustomed to the abbreviation that we can read it easily and correctly. But "yr." can be read as "your" or "year." Often the context indicates the correct reading, but in some cases one can only guess. On the other hand, writing in consonants alone was natural and quite tolerable from the Semitic point of view. Even in modern times, such Semitic writing as Hebrew can be understood both in print and in handwriting, without the use of vowel signs.

To help themselves, the Semites found ways of giving at least a hint about some of the vowels. If they meant an *o* or a *u*, they wrote a *w*, and a *y* for an *e* or *i*. This system was never meant to indicate all the vowels exactly. It was used only in some cases to give a rough indication of the vowel sound by means of so-called "weak consonants." We may, therefore, regard these attempts at indicating the vowels as leaving unaffected the basic nature of the Semitic script, which has remained consonantal.

The ancient Greeks also found the lack of vowels an inconvenience, but they went much further and, using some of the Semitic signs for consonants which the Greek language did not have, they soon built up a complete group of signs for all their vowels, and these they used as regularly as the consonants. And that was the way the first complete alphabet came into being.

Now the vowels, as we know, are made mostly with the open mouth. For the consonants, tongue and lips and teeth play a greater part. One cannot tell a vowel from a consonant by its symbol or sign. The letter called *'āleph,* for instance, was pronounced as a consonant by the Semites. The Greeks gave it the sound of the vowel *a*.

Of course, we are getting ahead of the story of writing. However, it is well to understand at the very beginning that vowels and consonants were not spoken in the same way for all languages nor used in the same way for all systems of writing. Otherwise most of us will be confused every time we examine a chart of letters. Remember that the sign or symbol for a letter is not the important thing. It is the way a sign is pronounced in any given tongue.

It should also be emphasized that the charts of letters given herein may well differ from charts found in other books because the dates of the alphabets may differ. The alphabets of Greeks, Etruscans and Romans alike changed with time so that the charts of their letters will differ substantially for the early and later forms of each.

In the letter charts, the sound values indicated are in some cases approximate. In this connection it would seem appropriate to comment on the sound value of the semitic *'āleph* and *'ayin.* *'Āleph* is a noise made in the throat when one begins to pronounce any word that seems to start with a vowel. There is no equivalent in English script. *'Ayin* is a hard sound made in the throat. English speakers cannot pronounce it but any Arab can do so.

CHAPTER TWO

Preliminary Stages of Writing

The horse and buggy age has disappeared, the Model T Ford is a museum piece, the propeller plane is giving way to the jet, the jet to the guided missile, and ways of writing have been improved. But the devices used by man to communicate with his fellow man before he learned to write are still with us today, and not in museums.

Such devices have a real value and a real part in the story of writing. They have been used throughout the ages, sometimes in place of the written word and sometimes in combination with the written word, such as a railroad sign with a flashing light and the word "stop."

Obviously the main function of memory devices

was to aid memory and they were employed by primitive peoples all over the world.

One of the earliest was the notched stick. A savage warrior wanted to keep a record of his prowess, so he made a nick or scratched a mark on his spear for every fallen enemy—just like the notches on the western six guns. Or primitive man made a kind of calendar with a notched stick, the kind of calendar, we are told, that Robinson Crusoe kept on his desert island.

A similar method was the use of knots instead of notches. Knots are not far removed from the knot tied in a handerkerchief to remind us of some duty to be performed. A simple application of these knots was in keeping a record of numbers. It is said that a savage hunter often left a knotted string with his wife to show her the number of days he would be away and to remind her that he would bring home meat for a feast on the day she untied the last knot.

Herodotus relates that even a mighty monarch used this crude device. Darius, he said, left with a guard at a bridge a thong with a number of knots equal to the number of days that their watch over the bridge should continue. One knot was to be undone each day and, if the king had not returned by the time all of the knots were undone, the guard was to break down the bridge and go away.

In our own hemisphere the Incas of Peru had their *quipu,* a device so ingenious that they were able to keep a fairly accurate record of their amazing empire. Another contrivance, familiar to us all, was the wampum belt often called the shell money of the North American Indians. Long accounts have been written about each.

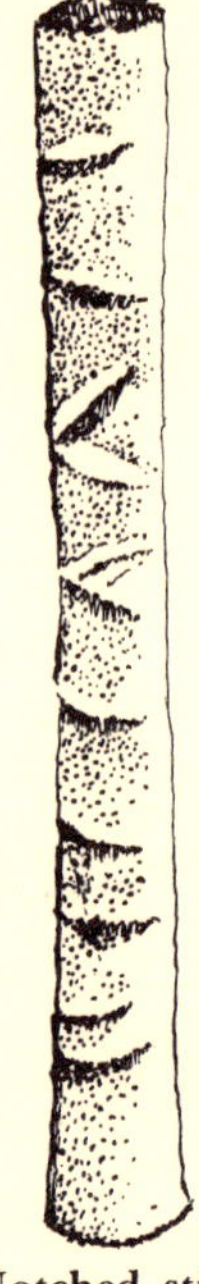

Notched stick

A quipu from Peru

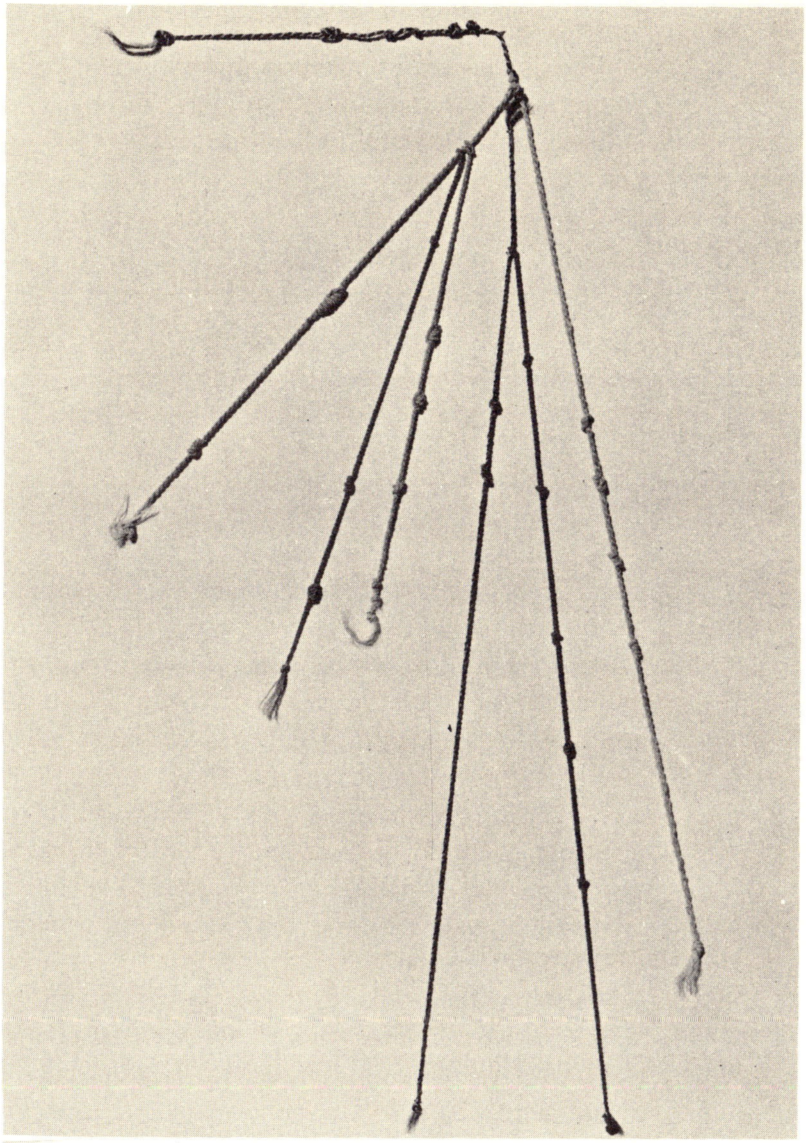

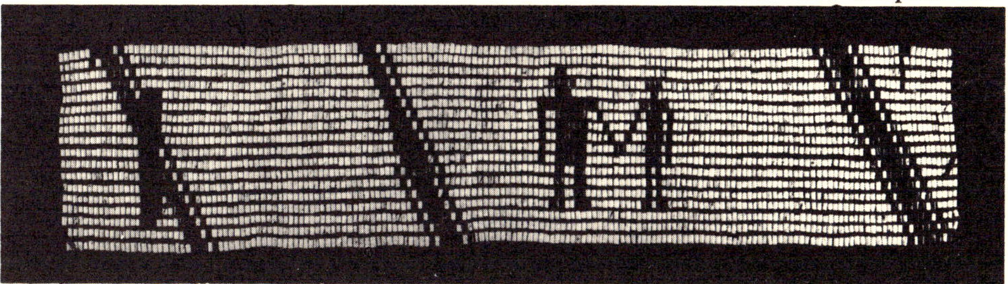

Courtesy of the American Museum of Natural History, New York

Famous Penn wampum belt

From the Collections of The Historical Society of Pennsylvania

The *quipu* had knotted strings and these knots were tied in a manner to designate numbers in a decimal system similar to our own.

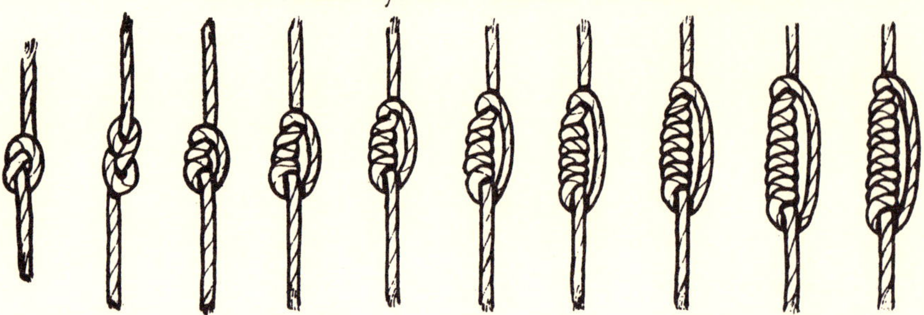

By Erland Nordenskiöld

Knots used on Peruvian quipus

In the place of knots the makers of wampum used shell beads. The Incas made use of colored strings, the Indians of colored beads. The colors had a meaning, just as today black stands for mourning or death and red for danger.

Both the strings and the beads served as memory aids for the recording of events, but it was no easy task to read them. It took wise men to interpret the meaning of knot and bead and color, so the Incas and Indians had men trained to memorize their meanings and read aloud the story of *quipu* and wampum.

As might be expected, *quipu* and wampum, in common with notched stick and knotted string, were also used to send messages. It would have been helpful if each notch or knot, or bead or color always stood for a certain word and had the same meaning. Since that was not the case, it was necessary to give the messenger a careful explanation of each thing he was to remember. It goes without saying that a messenger had to be a man strong in body. He had to be a man strong in memory as well, if his message were not to be garbled on delivery. No doubt, jumbled messages caused untold troubles in the ancient past; indeed, they may have changed history now and then.

But there were simpler ways of communication, of transmitting thought. Symbolic devices were quite popular. Some of them might even be called "talking things," for they spoke a language of their own—clear, precise, and not to be misunderstood.

If a tribe wanted to declare war on another tribe, they would send a spear or an arrow. It was clear to anybody that this smelled of blood. If it were a question of peace, the North American Indians sent a pipe. A pipe spoke of peace, a spear talked of war, and a drawn bow shouted: "We attack."

Pipe of peace

Other symbolic devices became well known through usage and are familiar to us in this twentieth century. From early days a ruling monarch wore a crown and we associate a crown with a king or his queen. For centuries upon centuries the cross has stood for Christianity. The blazon of a family, the coat of arms of a country are, with us, symbols which must not be altered, lest they lose their significance. Disrespect shown to a nation's flag is felt to be especially shocking.

Although small loan companies have put most pawnbrokers out of business, the three golden balls hung outside his shop remain the emblem of the pawnbroker's trade. Another symbolic device not often seen today is the white barber's pole with its red spiral, which was the image of the red bandage used to tie up a bleeding arm or leg. It was originally the emblem of a barber surgeon, but the barber continued to use it although he no longer bled his clients.

If the idea of a minstrel alongside a notched stick seems strange, it is not surprising, for the mere mention of storytellers in connection with writing seems at first farfetched. Still we must admit that they do have their place in the world's literature. Literature began when oral tradition and folklore were committed to writing.

In early times there was nothing like a "reading public." Nevertheless, as we do today, people loved stories and they enjoyed their stories not by reading but by listening. The ancient bards were really living books. They could recite for hours without pausing or losing their place in the tale.

Minstrel with harp

From the tales they recited we learn something about the history and religion of early peoples, about their heroes and their gods. Also, we know something about the court life and the home life of the people whose stories they chanted to the strumming of harp or lute or lyre. To them we owe our unwritten literature without which our written literature would be the poorer.

Do not smile condescendingly upon prince and noble who enjoyed their stories by listening because they could neither read nor write. Nor should one scoff at such crude devices as notched stick or knotted colored string. If we poke around in the odd corners of our minds while walking along the street or sitting at home, we shall find sudden, surprising examples of every device used by man before he began to write.

Take a few:

Has not the ordinary rosary much in common with ancient memory aids? For illiterate man, colors were used as one means of communication and today the familiar traffic light tells you more quickly than the written word to stop or to go. Can sailors get along without lights for starboard or port? Not well. Without benefit of words or letters, flowers carry a message of cheer and sympathy to the sick. A white flag signals its message of truce or surrender.

Those who tell stories to children do not think of themselves as modern bards. But are they not close kin to the ancient bard whose skill lay in the accurate recitation of favorite stories and epic poems? Nor do children differ much from the ancient bard's audience. They listen with rapt attention and demand accuracy in the repetition of each favorite story. Change one word and you will be promptly corrected.

Sign language of various kinds was widely distributed over the world. It was used as a primitive medium of communication among many peoples in early times and differed from area to area much as does the spoken language. One widely used sign language was that of the American Plains Indians when many Indians of various languages were in relatively frequent contact.

But like other methods of communication which have been found useful, sign language has not been discarded. We shake a fist at an enemy, raise a hat to a friend, shake our head for "no" and nod for "yes." Casino *croupiers* have developed a complete system of sign communication. The flirt-language of the fan, used by lovers in past centuries, conveyed fairly complicated messages.

These are just a few examples of the many devices which are used or have been used in place of writing. The curious reader will find it an interesting game to think of some on his own.

CHAPTER THREE

Picture Writing

Practically all systems of writing can be traced back to picture-writings. As we shall see, our own letters were originally pictures. Having been conventionalized, simplified and passed through many hands, they lost their pictorial character and reached their present forms—which are actually arbitrary.

This history of our alphabet could begin with the Sumerian pictures on clay or with the Egyptian hieroglyphics five thousand years ago, or it could begin thousands of years earlier than that with the art of the cavemen. Drawings probably existed even before those of the cavemen. (It is a general rule that the earliest known find is not necessarily the earliest occurrence.) At one time, before the cavemen's paintings were discovered, most people thought that art had originated in Mesopotamia and Egypt.

Picture-writings are found everywhere. They are the work of ancient peoples, the prehistoric inhabitants of Egypt, Mesopotamia, India, Crete, Europe and many other places, and of more recent peoples in Africa, Australia and the Americas. Picture-writing probably developed independently among various peoples on various continents at various periods of time. This means that the picture-writings of all peoples did not develop in exactly the same way and at exactly the same time. Picture-writings are not necessarily similar nor are they necessarily sequential in their development all over the world. When we consider the vast differences in the pictures and writings of peoples today, it would be surprising if they were.

Within the framework of this short book it is impossible to discuss in detail and chronological order the mass of pictures and symbols left by people from all over the world. For the sake of brevity it seems reasonable to start with cavemen of the Stone Age and, in order to illustrate various points in the development of picture-writing, to select appropriate examples from such places as Africa and North America without regard to the age, period or cultural stage of the people by whom they were produced.

In picture-writing the emphasis is on the picture or symbol and thus the meaning can be expressed orally in any language. It is independent of language. How then did picture-writing develop into what we call writing?

The general nature of the process is clear. Picture-writing evolved in two stages. The first, or most rudimentary one, is known as pictographic, the second as ideographic.

A pictograph (or pictogram) may be defined as a picture or symbol representing the object or thing shown. These drawings can also be called petrograms if they are drawn or painted and petroglyphs if they are incised or carved on rock, but, to avoid confusion, we shall use the term pictograph as all-inclusive. An ideogram may be defined as a picture or symbol representing not so much the things shown as the underlying idea associated with those things and doing so by suggestion.

The term pictograph thus applies when a picture represents nothing more than the object it portrays; if, for example, we draw a circle with rays to express the sun, this is a simple pictorial  sign or pictograph. But this pictograph becomes an ideogram when it no longer represents the object depicted but an idea associated with the object; when the circle with rays no longer signifies the sun, but light or heat or day. The picture of a foot may not only indicate a certain part of the anatomy, it may also give the idea of walking.

Try as others have, however, to define clearly and exactly these two stages of picture-writing, the same picture or symbol may be called a pictograph by one author, an ideogram by another. The line of demarcation between them is almost invisible because pictographs gradually evolved into ideograms. However, some say that the term logogram (word picture) is more appropriate than the terms pictograph and ideogram and that a better name for picture-writing would be word-writing or logographic writing.

To the layman this controversy may seem to be a matter of terminology. To the scholars it is a much more serious matter, as shown by I. J. Gelb, a prominent advocate of the logographic writing theory.

In his book, *A Study of Writing,* Gelb states that "In connection with the controversy 'ideography vs. logography', which is now raging in philological-linguistic circles, it may be worthwhile to note the following: All the Sumerian and Akkadian grammars use the term 'ideography', with Falkenstein, Friedrich and Poebel forming a small but notable group of objectors to that term. The Egyptologists, as one man, favor 'ideography'."

Without going into the arguments advanced for use of the terms logogram and logographic writing (and they are quite persuasive), it would seem appropriate herein to hold to the traditional theory of picture-writing by means of pictographs and ideograms until the logographic theory has received general acceptance.

As stated above, pictographs gradually evolved into ideograms, so to draw a sharp line between them may well cause confusion and debate. But no confusion need exist if we confine our story to the probable series of steps which were taken in the development of picture-writing, without referring to each step as a "thing-picture" or an "idea-picture."

The best known of the paintings and drawings

made by primitive man are to be found in prehistoric caves and rock shelters where Stone Age
man was driven for shelter from the cold and wild
beasts. It does not follow that primitive men were
artists only when they were in caves. The caves
are simply the places where their paintings and
drawings have been preserved, since they were
protected from the elements.

For his first pictures, primitive man seems to
have used the point of a flint tool to scratch crude
drawings on bits of stone and on the bones of wild
animals he had killed.

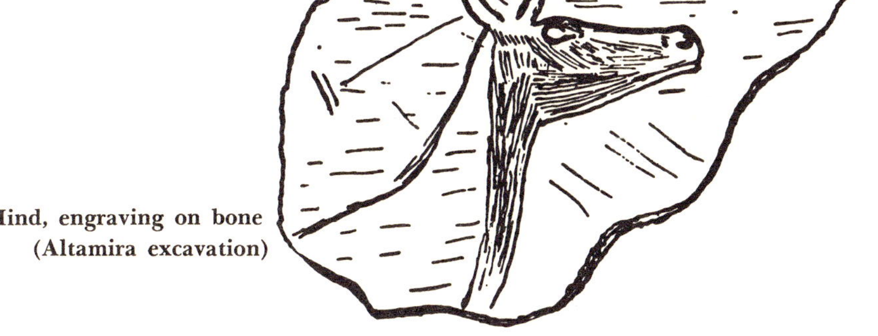

**Hind, engraving on bone
(Altamira excavation)**

He also worked on the surface of rock, on wood,
bark, animal skins, everything—not excepting
himself. It is still the custom of many tribes to
tattoo their bodies with pictures.

Man produced fine artists even in those remote
times when the mammoth and reindeer were
roaming around where Paris now stands. The
variety of the subjects they left behind is immense
—animals of all sorts and human figures in various attitudes and actions. Often the pictures are
sketchy and incomplete but many are wonderfully
distinct and clear.

Men of the Stone Age were a race of great hunters. They lived in an environment dominated by mighty wild beasts and everything was focused upon the quest for game. Nothing could have been more important to the Great Hunter than animal life, so he first turned to the drawing of animals—bulls, bison, deer, boars, bears and so on. These presumably were food staples and therefore favorite objects of the chase.

His earliest pictures of animals show them just standing, merely portraits of them; sometimes the whole beast was painted, sometimes only an outline was drawn.

A long step towards picture stories was taken when the artist showed the animals in action. Shown here are a galloping horse and a group of swimming stags.

Galloping horse, pierced by arrows *

Swimming stags *

Later on his pictures began to include people. Like the first animal pictures, they showed no action, just people standing or sitting or lying down. Such a drawing said no more than "This is a man." Again, as with animal pictures, the whole person might be shown, sometimes only an outline.

At last the pictures of people show action too. Men and women were drawn running, hunting, fighting. Now people became part of the picture story.

Women running *

Were prehistoric paintings and drawings done solely for purposes of religion and magic? Were these dark caves some sort of ancient temple where the elders of a tribe came to bewitch the animal images so that the hunter might be successful in his search for food? Were they used as visual aids to teach young hunters where to strike their prey in a vulnerable spot?

Prehistoric elephant with heart painted in *

Pictures could be treated under the history of art, the history of magic, or the history of writing. Speculate as you will, there should be little doubt that all were not made simply to please the eye. Some may have been "art for art's sake," but others may have been intended to have a meaning—some for magic and religion, some to commemorate an important event; still others are what we might call reporting on such matters as where to procure food and the like.

A picture of a crouching lion may look like a work of art, but it may have been intended to

* *From* THE ART OF THE STONE AGE *edited by Hans-Georg Bandi. Used by permission of Crown Publishers, Inc.*

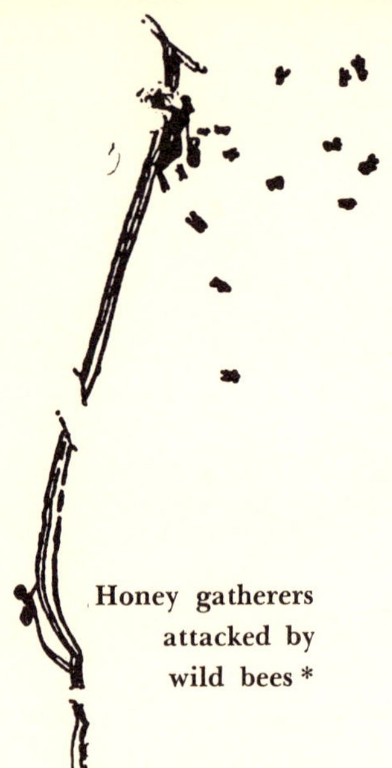

Honey gatherers
attacked by
wild bees *

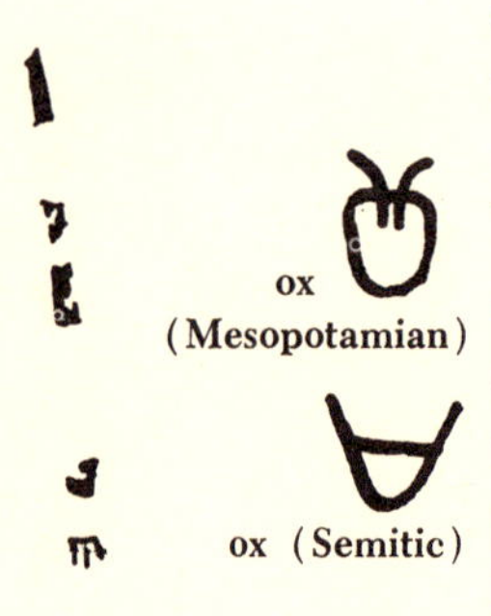

ox
(Mesopotamian)

ox (Semitic)

show that there were savage animals in the area. If primitive man drew a hunting scene, it probably served as a guide for food animals in his area, the way to hunt them, and the weapons used. Again, a battle scene would probably be intended to commemorate a great victory of the artist's tribe.

This picture of honey-gatherers climbing up a rope to the hiding place of wild bees and being attacked by them may have been just another guide with warning to delectable food. However, could it not also show that some of the primitive artists possessed a sense of humor?

But picture-writing, as we have seen, did not stand still. Man began to speculate on ways to represent an object with the very minimum of strokes, which might be called ancient shorthand. Thus the picture of an ox was reduced to a simple symbol by the people of Mesopotamia and to another variation by the Semites. The symbol for man differed somewhat in its treatment by various peoples, but it was generally reduced to a dot for the head, and lines for limbs and body, as shown in these examples from distant places.

South Africa

Sweden

North America

So early picture-writers everywhere discovered that they could express many different things with their pictures or symbols. They found that they

From THE ART OF THE STONE AGE edited by Hans-Georg Bandi. Used by permission of Crown Publishers, Inc.

could give character to their pictures by adding characteristic features, as in Indian symbols for man: a spear for a hunter, a cane for an old man, only one leg for a cripple, and many others.

The sun, as you will recall, might be represented by a circle, or by a circle with rays, and the use of a wavy line for water seemed to be quite common. Likewise the symbol for mouth could be a simple drawing of two lips. But the symbols for sun, water, and mouth were not always exactly the same among all peoples.

But even these simplified pictures had a serious disadvantage. They could represent many things but not everything. It was easy to make a symbol stand for things which can be seen: for man or ox, for water or mouth. But how could one represent things which cannot be seen? How, for instance, could the wind be drawn; or an enemy; or bravery; or weeping, eating, drinking?

Some people got out of this difficulty very cleverly. They could represent the wind by an inflated sail. And what is more natural than for the symbol of a lion or an eagle to have the meaning of bravery? Or for an arrow to stand for enemy?

And an artist was able to express other ideas by a skillful combination of two or more pictures. The classic example of this is the drawing of an

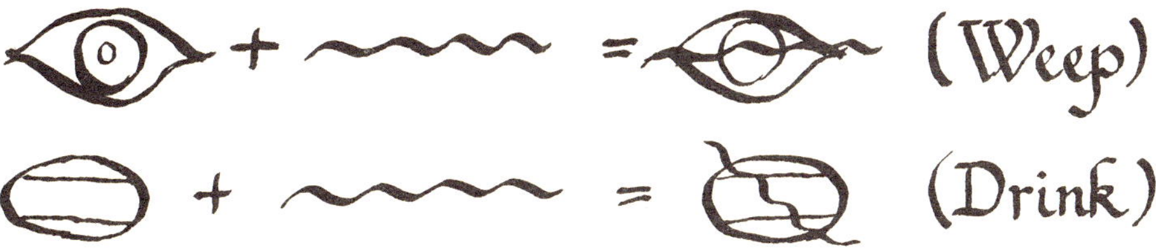

eye with tears dropping from it to express sorrow. Add water to eye and we have weep. Add water to mouth and we have drink.

It is clear that more complete stories became possible with these idea-pictures but, as already pointed out, it is a mistake to suppose that ideograms were suddenly used instead of pictographs. Both were used and they continued to be used side by side for centuries.

The American Indians' use of pictures to convey messages is well known. Each little picture or symbol represented an idea or a thing. Together they told a story, if the reader guessed right and filled in where necessary. Here is a famous museum specimen.

THE ROMANCE OF WRITING by K. G. Irwin

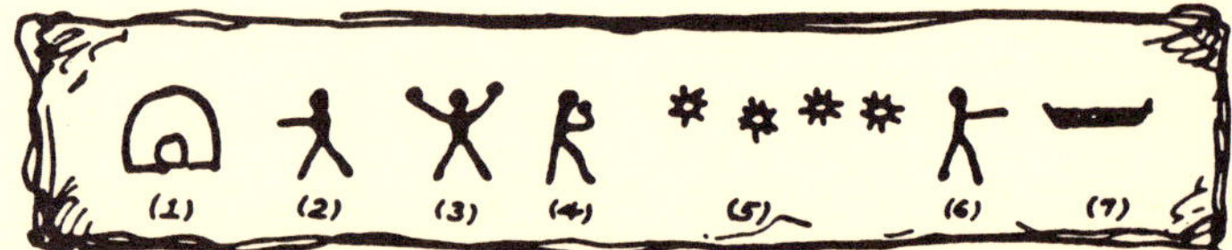

Indian message: *In the hut (1)   nothing (2)   to eat (3)   and drink (4)   We go 4 days (5)   in this direction (6)   by boat (7)*

However, writing by means of pictures or symbols was a form of writing which was intelligible only to the instructed and difficult for strangers to interpret. Three readers may interpret the same writing and get three entirely different messages.

At this point some person may comment to himself that alphabetic writing has the same weakness. Otherwise why should it be necessary to take letters and written agreements into court for judge or jury to determine their meaning?

However, for a disastrous example of this weakness, Herodotus tells about a message received by the Persian King Darius from the Scythians.

Darius interpreted the message to read, "O Persians, we surrender our land and our water (the mouse and the frog). We fly (the bird) from your might. We are ready to turn over to you all our arms (the arrows)."

Darius believed the Scythians had fled but that night they attacked and he learned that the true meaning of the strange message was, "Persians! Can you fly like a bird, hide yourself in the ground like a mouse, leap through the swamps like a frog? If not, you will die by our arrows."

Furthermore, picture-writing had another distinct disadvantage. The pictures or symbols might be drawn quite differently by different writers. They did not always use the same one for each idea or thing.

Thus, drink, as noted above, might be expressed by the picture of two lips for mouth plus a wavy line for water. In the Indian message it is drawn in another way. Again, the circle symbol for sun might be used by one writer to mean day, by others, to stand for heat or light.

drink (Indian)

Not only did writers differ in their ways of writing, but as civilizations grew up and life became more complex, ever increasing ingenuity was required to invent new idea-pictures. Some peoples advanced slowly to the final step where picture-writing developed into sound-writing by means of syllables or letters.

However, to conclude that writing followed a direct and unswerving course by stages which were mutually distinct would be misleading. Nor should we be deluded into thinking that man abandoned his picture-writing when the alphabet came into being. To be sure it had its disadvantages and its limitations, but man does not relinquish a serviceable tool or technique. He may improve upon it but he does not abandon it.

In more or less common use over the civilized world today is the pointing hand or arrow, meaning "Look there" or "This way."

If a bottle of medicine shows a picture of skull and crossbones, one immediately gets a complete message: "If you drink this, you will die." That message can be read by anyone, whether he has gone to school or not, and it can easily be understood by people speaking entirely different languages. But this is just another example of the fact that pictures did not always have the same meaning. In early days the skull and crossbones emblem betokened pirates to sailors of various nationalities even if they could neither read nor write.

Look around in bus or subway, thumb through advertisements in newspapers or magazines and note how the modern merchant uses pictures to advertise his goods.

Another interesting example of modern picture-writing is this device, which is a combination of ancient medical symbols for man, woman, and child.

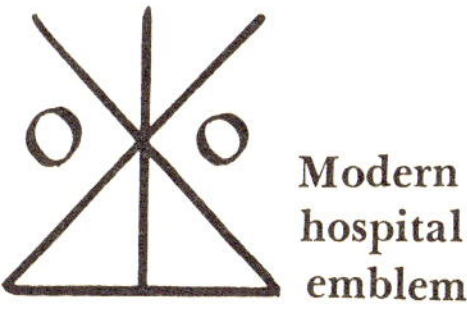
Modern hospital emblem

Children still symbolize hugs and kisses. A doctor's car is easily recognized by a small plate with a cross or caduceus on it. Saxon and Norman noblemen could not write their own names. They used instead the Christian sign of the cross. Illiterate John Doe of today does the same thing.

hugs

kisses

There is little doubt that pictures are being used more and more rather than less and less, and for a very simple reason. Authors can often tell more with a picture than with words.

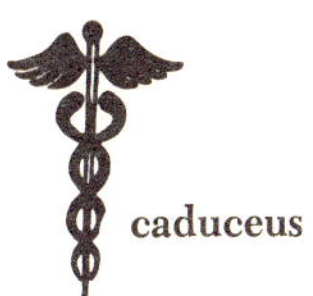
caduceus

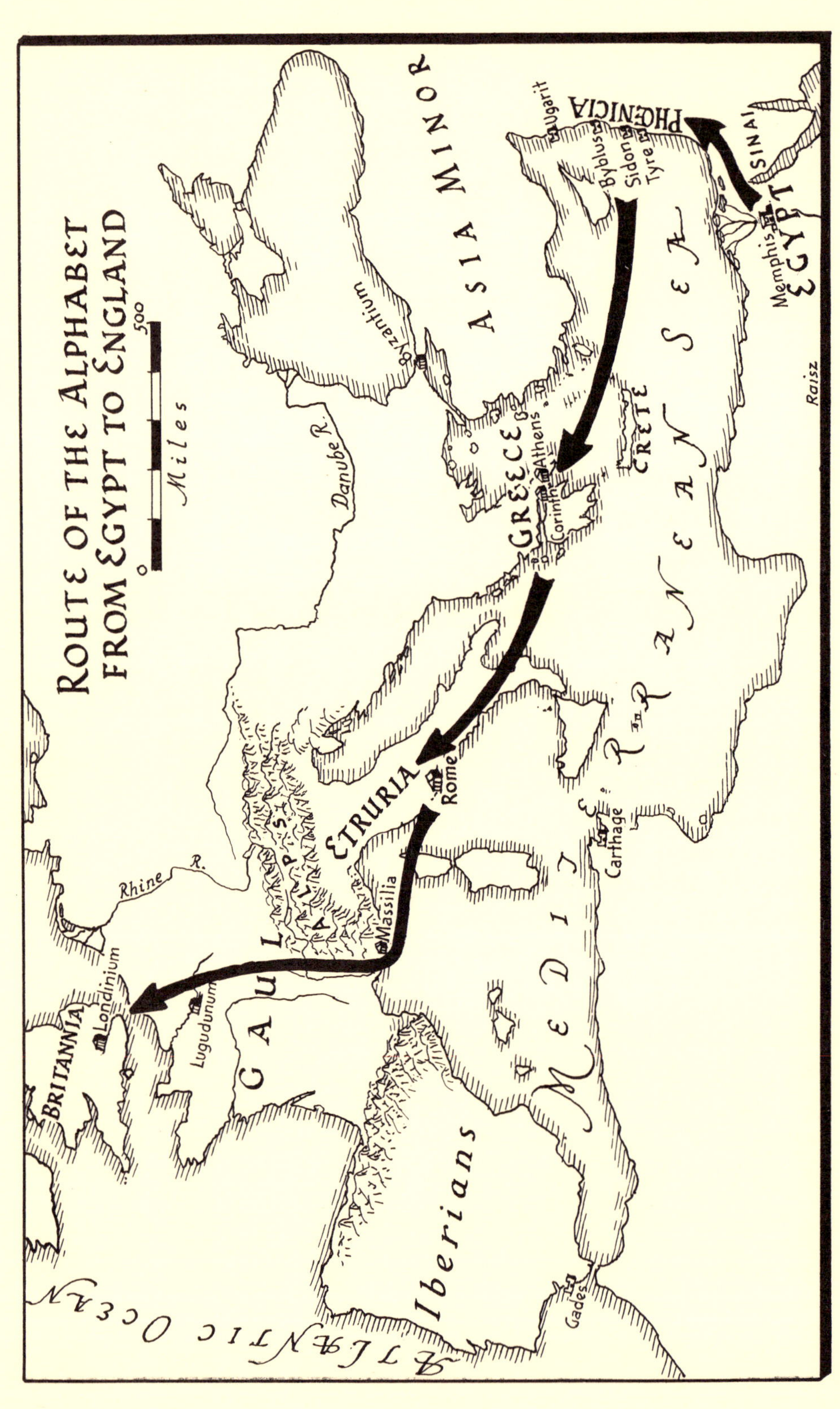

Route of the Alphabet from Egypt to England
Miles
500
0
ASIA MINOR
PHŒNICIA
Ugarit
Byblus
Sidon
Tyre
SINAI
EGYPT
Memphis
Byzantium
GREECE
Athens
Corinth
CRETE
AEGEAN SEA
Danube R.
ETRURIA
Rome
ALPS
GAUL
Massilia
Rhine R.
Lugudunum
Londinium
BRITANNIA
Iberians
Carthage
Gades
MEDITERRANEAN SEA
ATLANTIC OCEAN
Raisz

CHAPTER FOUR

Ancestry of the English Alphabet

After these brief surveys of the devices used for communication before writing began and of picture-writing, we now come to alphabetic writing. There are many different alphabets in use today. Some are used for one language only, some for several languages. But we are mainly concerned here with our own, which is in reality the Latin alphabet as adapted to the English language.

Perhaps its history will be more easily grasped if the reader is given an outline of its history at the beginning.

The following chart shows that the ancestry of the alphabet begins with the Egyptians. Some scholars have claimed that the Mesopotamians (cuneiform) and the Cretans (Linear B) have exerted an influence on the development of the alphabet; but there is no convincing proof for such claims. The Phoenicians are sometimes called North Semitic.

CHART OF ANCESTRY OF THE ENGLISH ALPHABET

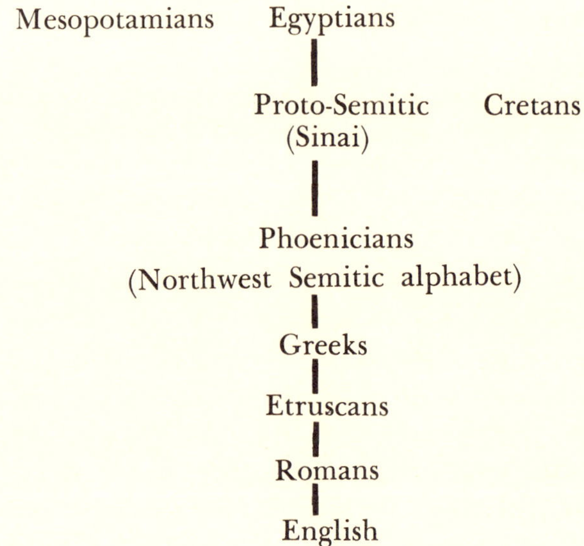

The map traces the route of the alphabet as it traveled from country to country over the ages, and from one people to another, until it reached the British Isles.

The ancestry of the English alphabet can also be given by showing the evolution of the letters from people to people. Take, for example, the letter *m*. The Egyptian hieroglyph for water stood for the letter *n* because their name for water began with the letter *n*. Of course the Egyptians and the Semites did not have the same names for the same things. The Semitic name for water was *mēm,* so when they took over the Egyptian water sign, they used it for the letter *m* instead of *n* and they changed the sign slightly. This letter and symbol were taken over by the Greeks, but they changed the name to *mu*. The Etruscans made a very slight change in the early Greek symbol and the Romans changed it to our letter M.

Egyptian   Semitic   Early Greek   Etruscan   Latin

The story of our alphabet from the time that we first find it employed in the earliest Greek inscriptions is not hard to trace. It is its history in pre-Greek days that is still wrapped in doubt. For a solution we might turn to stories of the divine origin of writing. The Egyptians attributed the creation of writing to Thoth or Isis. The Babylonian god of writing was Nebo. An ancient Jewish tradition considered Moses to be the inventor of their alphabet. But such a solution, of course, is entirely unacceptable.

How small was that part of the ancient world where the alphabet was born. The peoples seem to have been next-door neighbors. Indeed, each country situated in or near the eastern Mediterranean has been seriously considered to be the legitimate ancestor of the alphabet. And that is understandable, for thirty-five centuries allow plenty of time for experimentation with alphabetic writing and afford plenty of opportunity for various systems of writing, such as the Cretans', the Babylonians' and Egyptians', to contribute whatever they had to offer.

True, the Babylonians and Egyptians did not develop an alphabet in which each sign stands for one sound, but they did succeed in adding signs of purely phonetic value to their old ideograms. In other words, they developed writing systems which were a combination of idea-writing and sound-writing. And that was a tremendously important step.

Now we come to the most vital question in the whole history of writing. Who took that final step and became the inventor of alphabetic writing? To discuss the many theories which have been advanced would cause confusion where no confusion need exist because alphabetic writing is generally held to be a Semitic invention.

And that raises still other questions which agitate the scholars, for the term Semites does not refer to one particular group but to many peoples speaking the Semitic languages. These Semitic peoples included the Assyrians and Babylonians, the Aramaeans and the inhabitants of Canaan (Phoenician, Hebrew, Moabite), the Arabs and Ethiopians. Now just which one of these ancient peoples pointed the way for the Semites to make that last step in the art of writing?

The answers, as we shall see, may lie back in history when mines on the Sinai Peninsula were

Where our Alphabet was born

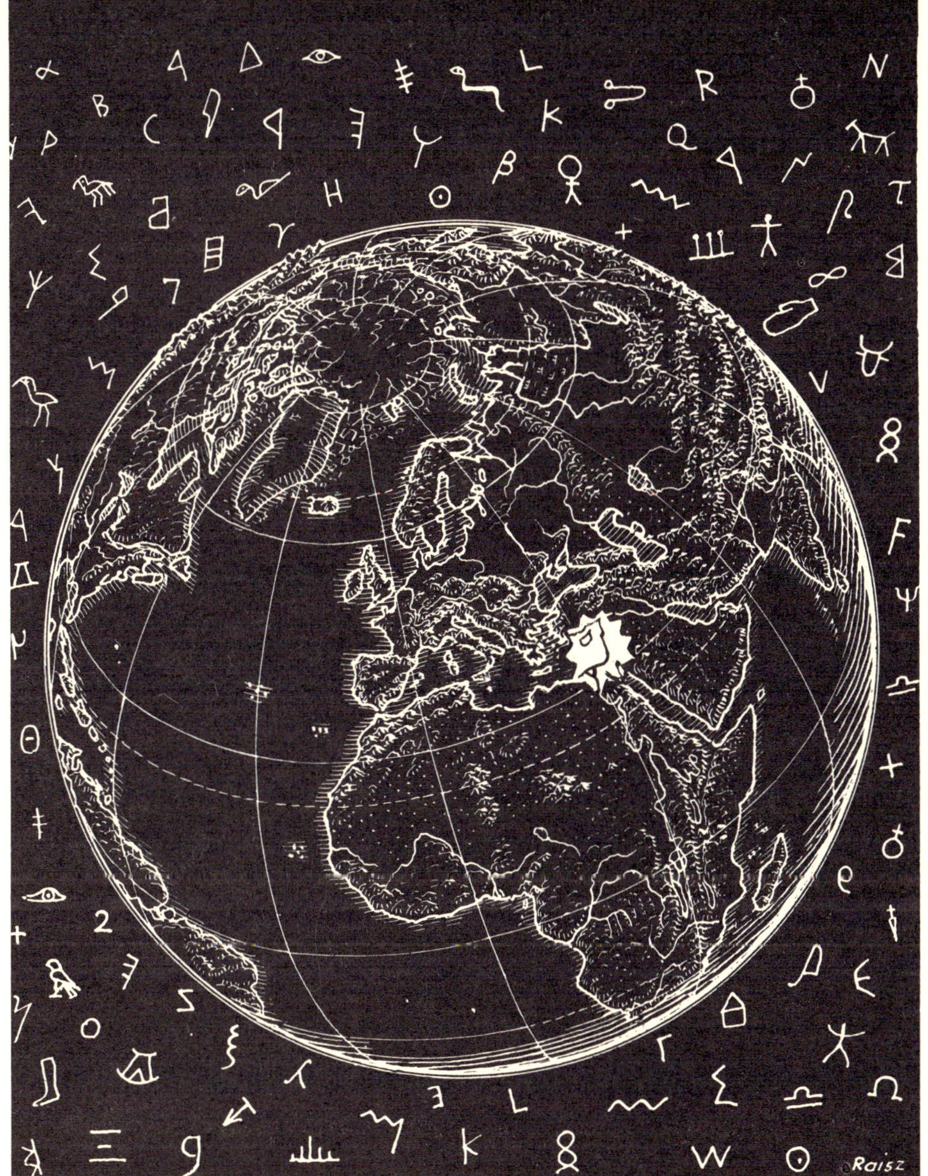

being worked by crews of local Semitic natives
under the direction of Egyptian officials. It does
not take a shrewd guess to imagine that the Egyptians must have brought their own system of writing with them to Sinai and that these ancient
Semites were intelligent enough to improve upon
the Egyptian way of writing.

The system of writing which they thus developed was a bare skeleton of some two dozen
consonants. From Sinai this primitive alphabet
seems to have been carried on currents of migra-
tion and trade through Palestine to the Northwest Semitic Phoenicians. While developing their
own alphabet, the Phoenicians may have been influenced by the scripts of other peoples, but the
Sinaitic origin of its beginnings seems to be a
reasonable assumption.

From Phoenicia the alphabet made its way to
the ancient Greeks, who added the vowels. From
Greece the letters crossed the sea to Italy. It was
not the Romans, as many seem to think, but the
Etruscans who were the dominant power in Italy
around the middle of the first millenium B.C.
From their hated rivals, the Etruscans, the up-
start Romans on the Tiber learned their letters
and improved upon them.

From Rome the Latin alphabet came to the
British Isles while at the same time spreading
throughout Europe. In short, our remote ancestors had to borrow from the Latins, who in turn
had borrowed from the Greeks, and the Greeks
themselves were indebted to the Semitic-speaking
peoples for their alphabet.

That Europe played no part in the invention

of what we call writing may seem strange because throughout Europe man employed his pictures to tell a tale or depict an occurrence. His stylized pictures, however, did not lead into the development of sound-writing as happened in Mesopotamia, Egypt and other countries where the learned and priestly classes took an active interest in such matters.

This outline of the history of the alphabet as it traveled to England would be incomplete without two important observations. One concerns the major role played by writing materials upon the shapes and appearance of the letters and signs used in the various systems of writing.

When picture-writing was beginning to develop from the drawings of cave dwellers, the materials must have been unbelievably hard to draw or write with. Man had no special materials, such as the pen and paper to which we are accustomed. He used anything and everything which could be used.

The peculiarities of each kind of material have always profoundly influenced the character of the writing done on them. And we shall find even greater differences in the appearance of the letters and symbols used for writing as they traveled from land to land and nation to nation—such differences as there are, for instance, between the wedge-shaped cuneiform jabbed into clay by the Babylonian scribes and the sweeping brush strokes on papyrus of the ancient Egyptian calligraphers. The pen, with its capability for curves, also eliminated the angular forms of letters.

The second observation concerns the influence

which the direction of writing had upon the shape and appearance of the written characters. We write and read from left to right and our letters face the way they do because the Greeks of about twenty-five centuries ago decided to have it that way. But that was not always so.

The ancient scripts were written in all kinds of ways: up and down, down and up; from left to right, from right to left. Sometimes the ancient scribes wrote alternate lines in opposite directions. This form of writing was called *boustrophedon,* which means ox-turning, as the ox turns at the end of each furrow when plowing. In such writing, the letters in alternate lines were reversed, so as to make them face in the direction of the reading.

The Hebrews and other peoples still write from right to left, which was the way some of the ancient scripts were written.

Hold a book in front of a mirror to see how the direction of writing changes the appearance of the letters.

Therefore, in order to understand better the charts of letters and writing signs given in the following chapters, it is essential to bear in mind not only the direction in which the people wrote but also with what tool and on what material.

Hittites
Hatti (Bogaz Köy)
ARMENIA
Armavir
Artaxata
Mt. Ararat
CASPIAN SEA
CAPPADOCIA
L. Van
MEDIA
Cilician Gates
Amida
Tarsus
Carchemish
MESOPOTAMIA
Nineveh
Arbela
Rhagæ
Euphrates
Tipsah
ASSYRIA
Ashur
Behistun
Ecbatana
Ugarit (Ras Shamra)
CYPRUS
Arvad
Palmyra
Tinga
Tigris
ELAM
PHOENICIA
Byblus (Gebal)
SYRIA
Sidon
Syrian Desert
Kit
Tyre
Damascus
Susa
CANAAN
Babylon
Kish
PHILISTIA
Pelusium
Gaza
Jericho
AKKAD
SUMER
Lagash
PERSIS
MOAB
Erech
EDOM
Ur
Eridu
present shore
Persian Gulf
Memphis
SINAI
Ezion Geber
EGYPT
Nile
MESOPOTAMIA
0
300
Miles
Raisz

CHAPTER FIVE

Mesopotamia

The history of writing now takes us to that part of the ancient world between the Tigris and Euphrates Rivers, the site of the fabled Garden of Eden. Over five thousand years of human history have unrolled in this land of Two Rivers. Today it is called Iraq and Baghdad is its capital. We shall call it Mesopotamia, for that is the name by which it has long been generally known.

Civilization first appeared here in the south, near the Persian Gulf, where the ancient Sumer was situated. Later, Babylon, on the river Euphrates, dominated the land, and Nineveh, the capital of Assyria further north on the river Tigris, in its turn ruled the country. On both of these mighty cities did the God of the Bible pour out His wrath.

A tourist of today can see no temples and statues as are on the classical ground of Greece; no pyramids rise towards the sun as in Egypt. Out of the deserts of Mesopotamia rise only mysterious mounds which show no visible trace of past greatness.

But these mounds, or *tells,* as the Arabs call them, kindled the imagination of inquiring spirits and the early explorers went to work with their spades. They were furious diggers and unearthed the ruins of great cities of the ancient world. Their discoveries lifted the curtain from the past and revealed that a culture as old as Egypt had flourished in the land of Two Rivers. It had risen in

Clay tablet with prayer to the goddess Ishtar

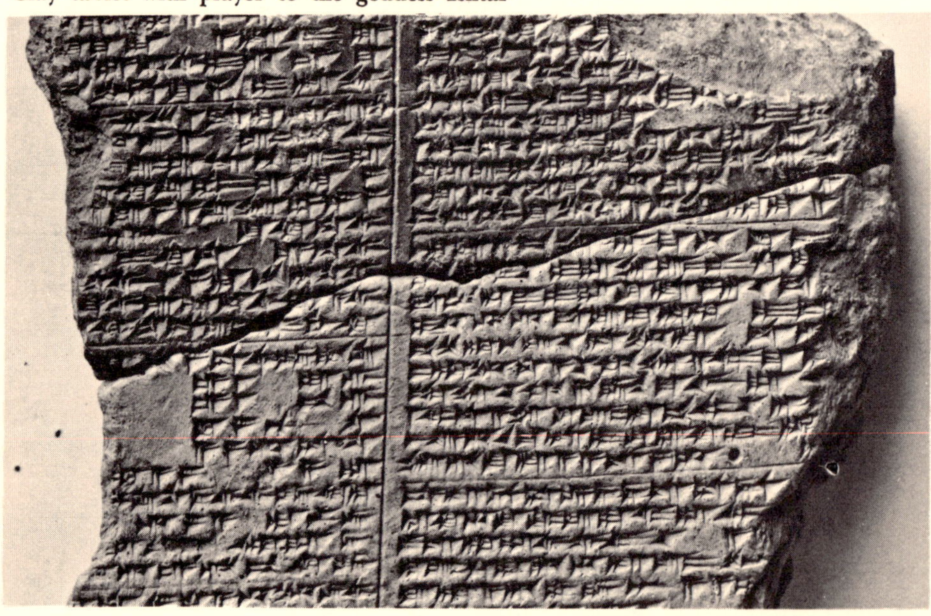

Courtesy of Trustees of the British Museum

might and splendor only to sink, under fire and sword, into oblivion, ignored by mankind for thousands of years.

Every tell proved to be a silent history book. How grateful are scholars of today that the ancient world knew nothing of municipal sanitation. Otherwise broken pottery, old armor, household tools and utensils, anything unusable, might have been cast away and destroyed.

The discovery of the first Assyrian palace was a newspaper sensation. People were amazed at the finds in the tombs at Ur of the Chaldees. But the clay tablets found in the ruins received no attention at first. And that was one of fate's little ironies, for these same clay tablets have proved to be the most important of all the discoveries made in Mesopotamia.

On these curious bricklike tablets writers jabbed little marks which looked as if birds had been walking on wet sand. Then they baked the tablets in a furnace or dried them in the hot sun so that they defied fire and flood and lasted down to our day.

It may sound unbelievable that such priceless treasures were almost lost to us and that it was the digger we have to blame. He was looking for more valuable things than insignificant clay tablets and was likely to ignore them completely. Indeed, he thought that the marks on them were just a sort of decoration and even threw them away with the rest of the dirt from his diggings.

How fortunate it was then for the history of writing when the peculiar marks were recognized to be a system of writing. Cuneiform it is called, from the Latin word *cuneus,* meaning wedge. What excitement, too, that discovery must have stirred among the students of history. No longer was the history of great civilizations and mighty empires, which had long since passed away, largely a matter of guesswork. Even the way the people lived emerged from the buried past on clay tablets, clay nail, prism and barrel.

These tablets of clay tell next to nothing about the inhabitants of Mesopotamia before the Sumerian outlanders moved into the land and became the founders of its first major civilization. That happened about 3000 B.C. From then on, the tablets tell about the countries of Sumer and Ak-

An inscribed clay "nail"
Courtesy of the Oriental Institute, University of Chicago

kad; about cities which were infinitely older than Babylon and the rulers of these city-states who became kings of Sumer and Akkad; about Sargon of Akkad, the first ruler who succeeded in uniting a large part of Mesopotamia under his power.

Centuries passed. Babylonia grew up and flourished where the kingdoms of Sumer and Akkad once stood. And we come to another familiar name of ancient history, to Hammurabi, the sixth king of Babylon. He, we learn from the clay tablets, founded an empire and was one of the great lawgivers of history.

Many more centuries passed. The power of Babylon declined. The warlike Assyrians to the

Clay prism of Sennacherib (left), barrels of Sargon (center) and of Nebuchadnezzar (right)
Courtesy of the Oriental Institute, University of Chicago

north were demanding their place in the sun. The armies of Ashur were marching forth to victory. That the Assyrians were an enterprising people as well as a nation of warriors is shown by their merchants, who, the tablets tell us, established a prosperous colony among the peoples of Cappadocia as far back as 1900 B.C. Cappadocia in Asia Minor was the home of the great Hittite Empire.

How many of us realize the debt we owe to these same clay tablets which have safely preserved for us the history of ancient Mesopotamia over a period of 2500 years? From them we learn about the Sumerians and Akkadians, about the Babylonians and Assyrians; of their rise and fall and rise again as they struggled for power; of the changing fortunes of various dynasties in the same country. We learn about the waves of invading Amorites, Kassites, Elamites, Aramaeans and others who seized power and lost it. And that is what we would expect of a land of many peoples and many tongues over so vast a period of time.

It is only necessary to know about two of the many tongues. The Sumerians spoke and wrote their own Sumerian language, which is very difficult for any foreigner to learn. When they were absorbed by the Babylonians, their language continued to be used in schools, and many a Babylonian schoolboy must have found it as difficult as modern schoolboys find Latin. The Babylonians and Assyrians were related people and spoke different dialects of one language. This is sometimes called Akkadian, or even Chaldean. The Akkadian language is a Semitic language, and the

Babylonians and Assyrians who spoke it were Semites.

There is much more, of course, that the clay tablets can tell about Mesopotamia, its people and their civilization. Important as this is to the historian, our interest lies in the story of writing. What is cuneiform writing? How does it fit into the development of our alphabet?

When they go back to the dawn of history, scholars are reluctant to state something as a proven fact. So it is with the date and origin of cuneiform writing. At first the Babylonians were thought to be the inventors. Later on it became clear that cuneiform script must have been handed down to the Babylonians by another people from an earlier age; that we must look to the more ancient civilization of the Sumerians. Whether or not the Sumerians started it we cannot say, but now it is generally accepted that it was they who developed this peculiar form of writing centuries before the Babylonians appeared in the forefront of history.

When the Sumerians settled in Southern Mesopotamia they did not know writing. They hunted animals, caught fish, and grew food crops on the fertile soil. Barley was the main crop, and to grow this it was necessary to irrigate the land, because there was almost no rainfall. The whole community worked together like a single family. They all helped to build and maintain the dikes, and when the crops were harvested they were taken to central granaries and rations were paid out as wages. This required records to be kept, since no one could remember how much barley had been paid out to every citizen of the community during the previous month. So writing was invented at first for bookkeeping, but later the Sumerians used it for other purposes as well. Paper and parchment were as yet not invented, so the Sumerians used clay, which could be got almost anywhere by digging down into the ground. The scribes, who were a specially trained group of men, held the clay in their left hands and wrote on it with their rights hands.

At first they drew pictures on the soft clay using a piece of reed with one end cut to an edge as the drawing implement. The pictures represented objects: A rough sketch of a bird or fish stood for these things, and the head of an ox stood for the whole animal.

CUNEIFORM PICTOGRAPHS

ORIGINAL PICTOGRAPH	EARLY CUNEIFORM	CLASSIC CUNEIFORM	MEANING
			bird
			fish
			ox

Then they began using pictures to represent ideas suggested by the picture: The rising sun stood for day. A sketch of a boomerang meant throw, and a foot meant walk and stand.

CUNEIFORM IDEOGRAMS

ORIGINAL PICTOGRAPH	EARLY CUNEIFORM	CLASSIC CUNEIFORM	MEANING
			sun day time
			boomerang to throw
			foot to stand to go

But the pictures were difficult to draw on wet clay.

Instead of drawing a perfect circle they pressed their stylus into the soft clay a number of times to make a rough outline of the circle. And since they held the stylus at an angle to the clay, just as you hold your pen sloping toward the paper, one end of the stylus went deeper into the clay than the other, leaving a wedge-shaped impression.

The wedges were pressed in several ways: perpendicular, horizontal, and oblique. To these was added another type of wedge which looked something like an arrowhead and was made with the tip of the stylus. These four types of wedges had to serve for all the pictures. No others were allowed.

Not only did the signs lose all resemblance to the pictures from which they originated but each could have more than one meaning. Thus the same sign could stand for a syllable, a whole idea, a word by itself, or indicate a proper name. But the scribes managed to solve that problem. To help the reader they would insert a special sign to show for what meaning the particular sign was being used.

These warning marks are called *determinatives* because they help the reader to determine the meaning of the word. They were generally placed before the word except in a few cases such as determinatives for place names and for birds.

CUNEIFORM DETERMINATIVES

city	land, mountain	objects of wood	objects of leather	(indicates a plurality)	places

The Babylonians took over the Sumerian writing and used it for their own Semitic language. The signs might mean a whole Babylonian word or just a syllable. They did have separate signs for the vowels *a, e, i,* and *u* (but no *o*), but they never had signs for the consonants. They could write *ab, ba,* or *a,* but they could not write *b* by itself. The reason is that you cannot pronounce *b* by itself, but only with a vowel. As a result the Babylonians and Assyrians never had an alphabet, but used a system of writing with more than 350 different signs.

SYLLABIC SIGNS

ab	en	si	bu
sag/rish	sar	tum	gam

No wonder writing was a special craft! To help themselves they made lists of signs with their meanings and compiled lists of difficult words with explanations. These were their dictionaries.

That these syllabic signs, which the Semitic Babylonians took over from the non-Semitic Sumerians, contain a clear and obvious vowel betrays their non-Semitic origin. Certain Semitic scripts had only consonants, not vowel sounds, and the Phoenician alphabet, as we shall see, consisted of twenty-two letters all of which were consonants.

Therefore, if it appears that the Babylonians borrowed an ill-fitting garment from the Sumerians, remember that a language and its writing are not necessarily the same thing. They do not always answer each other's needs. In fact, no writing system, not even an alphabet, is a perfect tool. Anyone who has gone through school knows what it is to learn English spelling with all the different ways of representing the same sounds and with so many unnecessary letters like the *e* in table.

In short, the Babylonians borrowed the cuneiform signs and applied them to their own Semitic language. The Babylonians did not originate their own writing system. They borrowed one and got along with what they took over from the Sumerians. They used the same signs but modified them to suit their own Semitic speech.

Nor were the Babylonians the only people who borrowed the cuneiform way of writing and adapted it to their own language. The Elamites in what is now Persia, the little known Urartians in the modern Armenia, the Hurrians in Syria and upper Mesopotamia and the Hittites in Asia Minor all borrowed cuneiform writing and adapted it for their own languages.

And the youthful scribe had his blackboard and eraser as well. He took a lump of clay, rolled it in his hands in the shape of a ball, flattened one side of it against a plane surface, and wrote on the flat portion. His work done, he rolled the tablet into a ball once more, flattened it again, and he had his writing material ready for the next trial.

Another thing employed by the people of

Mesopotamia was the cylinder seal rolled on the soft clay as a way of signing their names.

Courtesy of the Oriental Institute, University of Chicago
An ancient "signature"—a cylinder seal and its impression

If, as we have seen, the highest achievement of cuneiform was a syllabary, how then could cuneiform, as some scholars have suggested, have had anything to do with the development of our alphabet?

For one thing, Syria and Palestine, as the map shows so clearly, formed a sort of bridge uniting the great civilizations of Egypt and Mesopotamia. Traders were constantly passing through these countries and the lands changed hands a number of times. Clay tablets have been discovered in scattered places in both Syria and Palestine, testifying to constant Babylonian influence. Therefore it would seem likely that an alphabet invented by the Semites of Palestine and Syria was at least influenced by the Babylonians and their writing.

The tablets unearthed at Tel-el-Amarna in Egypt were letters written about 1400 B.C. They are the official diplomatic correspondence from the rulers of Palestine, Syria, Asia Minor and Mesopotamia to the Pharaohs of Egypt. They are in the language and cuneiform script of Babylonia because Babylonian was the diplomatic language of the ancient world. Thus, all evidence points to the use of cuneiform script by the Semites of Syria for diplomatic purposes at the time of the Tel-el-Amarna letters.

Just as the more backward peoples of Europe took up the Latin alphabet and adopted it for their languages, so the peoples surrounding Mesopotamia adopted for their languages the Babylonian method of writing. Just as Latin in the Middle Ages was the common language of scholars, so Babylonian became the common language of culture and diplomacy.

Cuneiform is not a direct ancestor of the alphabet, but many archeologists consider that the Sumerians first invented writing and that the Egyptians borrowed the idea from them and produced their own system. If this be so, the Mesopotamian system was the fountainhead of all Near Eastern writing.

And here our story of cuneiform ends, for the way it was deciphered is a long story by itself. Suffice it to say that a German professor, G. F. Grotefend, laid the basis for the decipherment about 1802, but Henry C. Rawlinson, a British diplomat, was possibly the greatest worker in the field. In 1846 Rawlinson published a translation of the Persian text of the Behistun Inscription, which recorded the achievements of Darius in three languages—Old Persian, Babylonian, and Elamite. A few years later Rawlinson tackled successfully the problem of the Babylonian writing, so he may be called the real "father" of the decipherment of cuneiform.

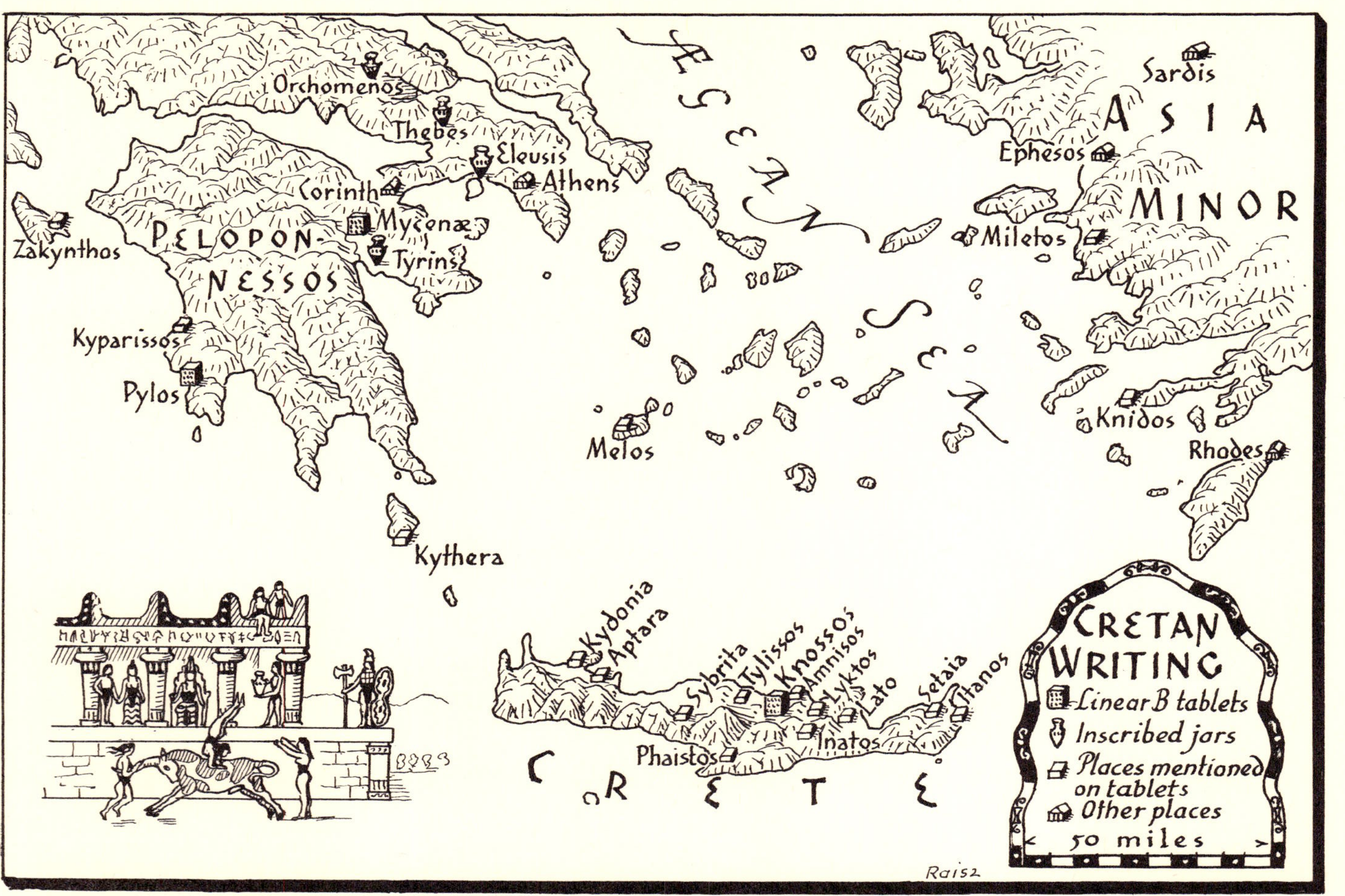

ASIA
MINOR
Sardis
Ephesos
Miletos
Knidos
Rhodes
ÆGEAN SEA
Orchomenos
Thebes
Eleusis
Athens
Corinth
Mycenæ
Tyrins
Zakynthos
PELOPON-
NESSOS
Kyparissos
Pylos
Melos
Kythera
Kydonia
Aptara
Sybrita
Tylissos
Knossos
Amnisos
Lyktos
Lato
Setaia
Itanos
Phaistos
Inatos
CRETE
CRETAN WRITING
Linear B tablets
Inscribed jars
Places mentioned on tablets
Other places
50 miles
Raisz

CHAPTER SIX

The Cretans

Cretan scripts do not appear to belong in the mainstream leading to our own alphabet. Thus, this chapter is placed here, rather than after the chapter on Egypt where it belongs chronologically. The Cretan scripts may or may not be directly influenced by Egyptian hieroglyphics. What is important is that the Phoenician or Semitic alphabet, which is ancestral to ours, stems out of Egyptian writing, and we do not wish to interrupt the story of that chain of development.

Nowadays the island of Crete belongs to Greece, but long ago, when the great civilizations of Egypt and Mesopotamia were flourishing, Crete did not belong to Greece. There was no kingdom of

Greece then—only a number of small, hostile states, struggling for power.

In her ancient heyday Crete was a cultural and commercial center for the Aegean Sea. Her civilization rivaled that of the Egyptians and Mesopotamians. Her palaces, factories and pottery works were famous, and her artists and sculptors were producing great works.

Cretan houses were sometimes five stories high with oil-parchment windows. Of more interest was her palace drainage system, which was far superior to anything known in the Western World during the following three thousand years and more. They drew their water through pipes from the hills by a siphon system which was unknown to the Romans, who could have made good use of it in their aqueducts.

Her wealth came from her strategic trading position and from command of the sea.

Cretan culture is often called Aegean because the civilization was shared with the islands of the Aegean Sea and the Greek mainland. It is also called Minoan after Minos, the legendary King of Crete and son of mighty Zeus. Later, after the rise of Mycenae on the mainland and the destruction of Knossos, it became known as the Minoan-Mycenaean culture, or simply Mycenaean, and spread through the eastern Mediterranean.

An English scholar, Arthur Evans, discovered the site of the ancient city of Knossos. In the popular imagination his great exploit was the excavation of the Palace of Minos, the dancing hall of Ariadne and the Labyrinth. For us, however, his importance rests not upon the works of art he discovered but upon the discovery at Knossos of clay tablets covered with mysterious writings.

Tablet from Knossos: Linear A script (left); Linear B script (right)

The oldest forms of Cretan writings, as happened in most other systems, consisted of pictorial signs for recognizable objects, such as a head, a hand and so forth.

This was the script of the seal stones, but Evans also found more advanced kinds of writing on clay tablets.

In the first, which succeeded the script of the seal stones and which Evans called Linear A, the pictorial signs are reduced to mere outlines. Then at some date which can not be precisely determined, Linear A was replaced by a modified form of script to which Evans gave the name of Linear B.

The relationship between these two linear scripts is perplexing. It is not, as one might expect, a matter of reducing the earlier signs to a simpler and easier written form. In some instances Linear B signs are more elaborate than their Linear A counterparts.

Unfortunately, no precise date can be given for the beginnings of Linears A and B or for the end of their use. But this much we can say: The Cretans wrote on clay, and clay tablets for both Linears A and B were discovered at Knossos, which was destroyed about 1400 B.C. Linear B tablets were found also amid the ruins of Pylos and Mycenae on the mainland.

A number of these mainland tablets deal with military and naval matters. The introductory phrase from one reads: "Thus the watchers are guarding the coastal areas."

An enemy landing from the seas was evidently feared, but a watchman slept or something else happened to bring complete destruction upon these ancient cities.

Since all three of the sites where Linear B tablets have been found were destroyed by fire, one might expect little of value to be left in their ruins. But that was not the case. Since the Cretans did not bake their precious clay tablets, the fire, though destroying many articles of utmost value for archeologists, actually preserved Cretan writing by baking the clay tablets to a hardness that made them last for three thousand years more.

Most systems of writing have had many books written about them, but until the last decade there hasn't been much about Cretan writing. Scholars wrote about Crete, to be sure, but they always concluded with a statement such as, "So far, the writing of Crete has not been deciphered." And that is the reason why all but the most recent books about Cretan writing are out of date.

Scholars needed another Champollion, the man

who had deciphered the Rosetta Stone over a century before. Around 1950, along came a young Englishman named Michael Ventris. From early childhood he had displayed a marked liking for mysterious scripts. Like Champollion, he had a great gift for languages and his interest in Cretan writing never flagged.

A study of the signs in Linear B led Ventris to the conclusion that Linear B must be a syllabic system of writing. According to John Chadwick, an associate of Ventris, "A count of all these signs shows that they number about eighty-nine—the exact number is still disputed. But even this number is significant; it is far too small for a wholly ideographic system, and it is much too large for an alphabet. Linear B must therefore be syllabic —and a fairly simple form of syllabary, like the Cypriote or the Japanese Hiragana system."

With the aid of Chadwick, Ventris accomplished the decipherment of the Linear B script in 1953. Yet even more exciting to scholars was their conclusion that the tablets were written in Greek—in a difficult, archaic Greek, but Greek nevertheless.

This is not to say that the language of Crete was always Greek. The young Englishmen had confined their efforts to Linear B, the latest script. Only when someone succeeds in deciphering Cretan hieroglyphs and Linear A shall we discover the language of the mysterious and legendary folk that settled in Crete.

Ventris started off with the thought that Linear B could be written in Etruscan. The very idea of a Greek language in Crete was forbidden by orthodox history and archeology. This staggering error cost him years of fruitless labor before he abandoned the theory that Etruscan words were the key to the decoding of Linear B. He and Chadwick had found far too many Greek words for it to be purely a matter of coincidence.

As might be expected, they met with outright skepticism from other scholars until an American, Carl W. Blegen, discovered a tablet from Pylos which proved to be a brilliant confirmation of their decipherment of Linear B and their conclusion that Greek was the language.

Inventory from Pylos of tripods and vases

To enter into a technical discussion of the decipherment and its confirmation is unnecessary. Our interest lies in the fact that the Pylos tablet contains an inventory of tripods and vases, some of which we can recognize. For instance, the jug with the three ears and the wine jar.

We can tell even the number of various vessels for, like us, the Cretans used a decimal system. Our numerical signs are an improvement over theirs, but theirs are quite adequate: vertical strokes for digits, horizontal strokes for tens, circles for hundreds, circles with rays for thousands and circles with rays and a central bar for tens of thousands.

digits

tens

hundreds

thousands

tens of thousands

Crete, as we know, lies like a stepping-stone to the doorsill of Greece. Could Crete have been a stepping-stone in the path of Grecian writing? Can we accept Linear B as the true ancestor of the Greek alphabet? The answer is quite simple since most scholars do not dispute the fact that the alphabet was invented by the Semites and that the Greeks borrowed their alphabet from the Semitic Phoenicians.

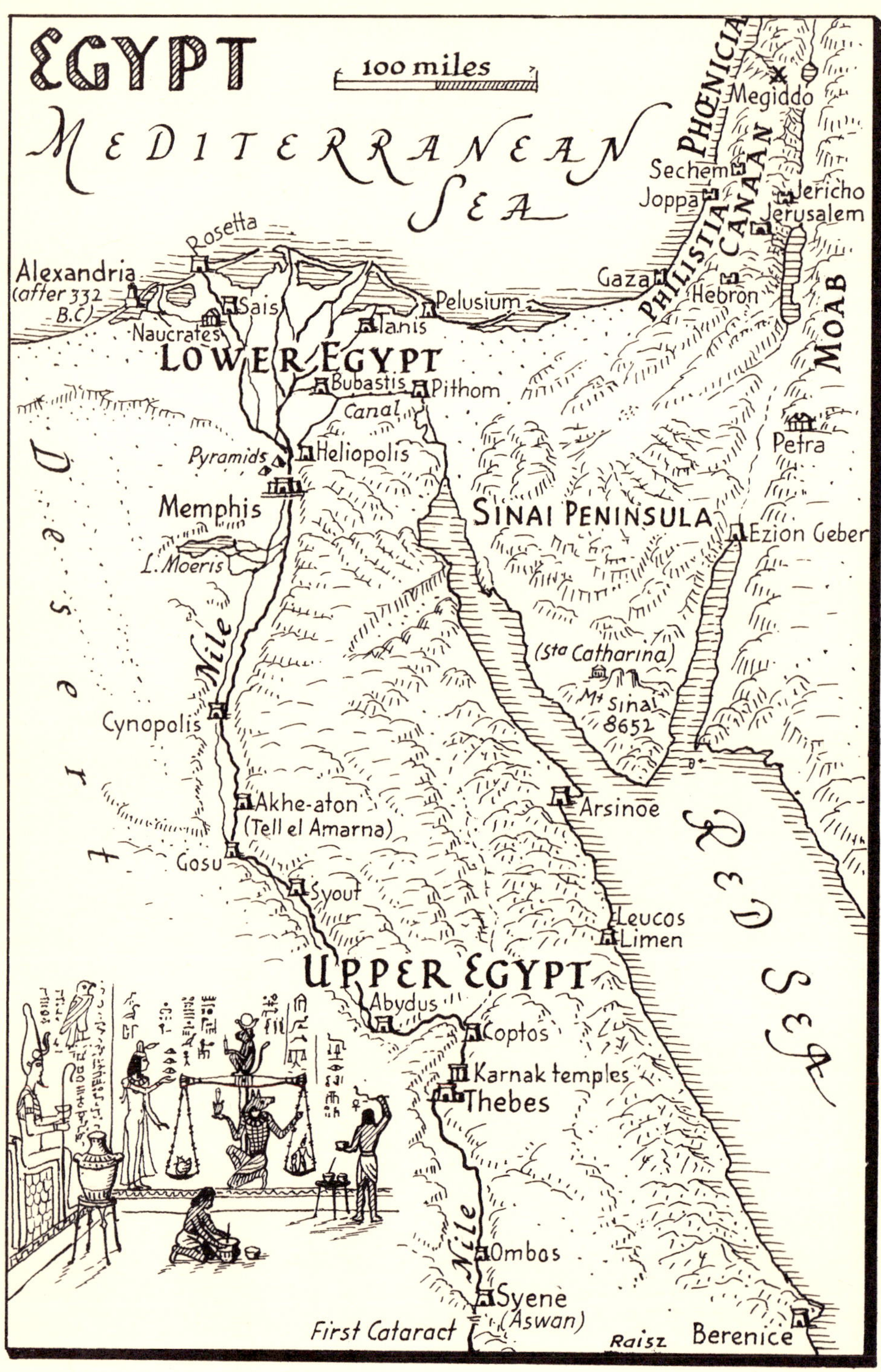

EGYPT
100 miles
MEDITERRANEAN SEA
PHOENICIA
Megiddo
Sechem
Joppa
Gaza
Hebron
CANAAN
PHILISTIA
Jericho
Jerusalem
MOAB
Rosetta
Alexandria
(after 332 B.C.)
Sais
Naucrates
Pelusium
Tanis
LOWER EGYPT
Bubastis
Pithom
Canal
Petra
Pyramids
Heliopolis
Memphis
SINAI PENINSULA
Ezion Geber
L. Moeris
Desert
Nile
(Sta Catharina)
Mt Sinai
8652
Cynopolis
Akhe-aton
(Tell el Amarna)
Arsinoe
Red Sea
Gosu
Syout
Leucos
Limen
UPPER EGYPT
Abydus
Coptos
Karnak temples
Thebes
Nile
Ombos
Syene
(Aswan)
First Cataract
Raisz
Berenice

CHAPTER SEVEN

The Egyptians

Egypt is old. She was already old when Romulus and Remus founded Rome. She was old and blighted when the Germans and Celts of the western European forest were still hunting bears. Unlike Mesopotamia, which was the other great power of ancient civilization, Egypt was a land of oneness—one river, one civilization, one people, one language, one history.

But the Egyptians, like all ancient peoples, did not leave us history books in the modern sense; nor did they reckon the flow of time from some fixed point. Instead for a time they dated in "King's Years," naming the years of each king after a prominent event that happened during them. Thereafter they numbered the year of each king. This muddled way of recording their history continued until an Egyptian priest named Manetho wrote a history of Egypt in Greek some three hundred years before Christ.

Brushing aside the usual legends of god-kings and heroes, Manetho started his history with Menes, who united Upper and Lower Egypt into one nation. Then, with about three thousand years of history to account for, he divided the long list of kings into thirty dynasties (or groups) of rulers.

His scheme of dynasties may seem strange to us, but in spite of its defects it has taken firm root and there is little chance of its being abandoned. It is still used today, and that is why we read that a certain thing happened in the first or some other dynasty. We read about the Old Kingdom, the Middle Kingdom, the New Kingdom.

Egypt was a land of oneness, a land of dynasties —and a land of monuments. For most visitors, her remote past is the magnet which draws them. For them, Egypt is a land of past glories, of pyramids and temples, of tombs and obelisks, of paintings and inscriptions, of the River Nile.

In the shadowless wastes the pyramids lift their heads. There the obelisks stand out needle sharp, guardians of temple gates. There, too, crouches the Sphinx of Gizeh.

There is no country that has kept shining secrets hidden so well for centuries. Where else could one find a Tutankhamen tomb? Before the diggers set to work, yellow sands, lying smooth and silent beside the long, blue river, gave no sign of brilliant pageants that had long ago passed along the Nile. Rock cliffs and valleys stood calm and blank under the blazing sun, never revealing a hint of the treasures they were holding.

Archeology has won its greatest triumph in Egypt. The reason is simple. The dry climate of that land, the very scanty rainfall and the sands which do not hold moisture have all collaborated to preserve the ancient treasures. Even filmy linen, textiles, furniture made of wood, the last food placed for the dead in the tomb by mourners—and hundreds of other things that bring us almost face to face with these long-ago men, women and children—have been preserved. The dry air of the Nile country has preserved, and the drifting sands have sealed in, what would have been destroyed or lost in another region.

Religion, too, has played an enormous part in the preservation of Egypt's past, for the ancient Egyptians surpassed all other peoples in the effort to provide their dead with all they might need in their future life. We would have little knowledge of the Egyptians if it were not for their faith in a glorious afterlife for their kings. Because of this belief, they built pyramids out of stone and had the bodies of their rulers embalmed to last, they hoped, forever.

All the pyramids were tombs but not all tombs were pyramids. Some tombs were just stone buildings with flat tops; some were simply caves, cut into the rock cliffs on the west side of the Nile so that the entrance would face east toward the rising sun. All were memorials to the Egyptians' belief in a life after death.

Architects erected colossal pyramids and magnificent columned temples. Sculptors and painters portrayed gods, humans and animals with admirable realism and grace. The people who once ruled the ancient kingdom march in endless procession across the narrating friezes, stiffly posed, breathing greatness in every gesture, always shown in profile and directed toward some goal. Every king was represented as a conqueror—both in reliefs on temple walls and in the ancient writings.

Trying to match the splendor of the tomb of their lord, the king's followers spent their wealth on tombs for themselves and their dead. Scenes from the tombs of rich nobles also tell of hunting and dancing and sport, but the scenes on the tombs of lesser men tell more about the people. We see flax being prepared, reapers mowing grain, and the melting of metal in simple kilns. The process of building a ship is illustrated; the felling of trees; the cutting of planks; the use of edge, handsaw and paring chisel. There are merchants selling necklaces and perfumes, oil cakes and fish, sculptors, stone masons and jewelers at their daily tasks. When we see these scenes we can easily picture to ourselves how an Egyptian workshop looked and how trading was done in the market place.

We read about a temple school where the priests gave courses in surveying, architecture, and medicine about four thousand years ago. And they also trained scribes in reading, writing and simple calculations. Copybooks survive with the corrections of the teachers still adorning the margins; the abundance of errors would console the modern schoolboy.

Copybook corrections

A simple fact strikes us again and again. Egypt would have kept her past intact if it had not been for the boldness of tomb robbers. In certain villages for centuries on end tomb robbing was a regular occupation. It seems almost uncanny that a papyrus document relating to a tomb robbery trial that took place three thousand years ago was found. Unfortunately that trial did not bring an end to tomb robbing.

However, despite the fascination and interest of these lost treasures, our interest lies in the Egyptian system of writing. Of importance to us is the fact that practically every object in this vast graveyard of the past was covered with writing. There were writings on the walls of temples and burial chambers, on memorial plaques and coffins, on statues of gods and mortals, on boxes and clay vessels. And from these records scholars have rebuilt the story of the past.

The Egyptians gave the world its first medical book; its first pharmacopoeia (including castor oil); its first instruction in surgery, in the diagnosis and treatment of disease, and in the use of bandages, compresses, sutures and splints.

The Egyptians seem to have been fonder of writing than any other ancient people. Above, below or at the side of painting and sculpture are words in their writing.

Courtesy of the Metropolitan Museum of Art

Wall painting with hieroglyphs

Until the beginning of the last century no one could tell what it meant. The picturesque writings of ancient Egypt had kept their secrets as silently as the Sphinx itself until a soldier of Napoleon found a slab of black stone during fortification work at the village of Rosetta near the western mouth of the Nile in 1799.

Courtesy of Trustees of the British Museum

The Rosetta Stone

The stone was about four feet long. On one polished side was an inscription written in three kinds of script: at the top, Egyptian hieroglyphics; in the middle, Egyptian demotic writing; at the bottom, Greek. The inscription was a priestly decree of the year 196 B.C. in honor of Ptolemy II, Epiphanes, but that was not particularly important. What was important was that the same thing had been written in three ways, and that one was Greek which could be read with ease.

How delighted the scholars were with that find! The Egyptians themselves had been of no assistance. Long ago the people of the Nile country had given up their own language for that of their conquerors. And when that happened their ancient system of writing was doomed. In a few centuries after the death of Cleopatra in 30 B.C., hieroglyphic inscriptions on tomb and temple wall meant no more to the literate Egyptian than they do today to the tourist passing through.

But with the Rosetta Stone scholars at last had a key to the mysterious hieroglyphics behind which were hidden centuries of history of the Egyptian people, their customs and ways. It seemed that all they had to do was to compare the Egyptian and Greek writing and the secret would be disclosed. But disappointments were in store. Deciphering the Rosetta Stone turned out to be a tremendously difficult task. No one knew whether the signs were words or letters or pictures.

For twenty years after the discovery, scholars worked hard but made little progress until an Englishman, Thomas Young, proved that at least some of the characters were letters of a sort, not just pictures, and with luck on his side managed to identify the name of Ptolemy. At a loss to make further headway, however, Young seemed content to leave the problem to someone else.

And so we come to the exciting part of the story of the Rosetta Stone. A young Frenchman, Jean François Champollion (1790-1832), appears prominently on the scene. Except for him, scholars might still be unable to read the ancient inscriptions. As a little boy he had been enchanted by his first sight of hieroglyphics on stone tablet and papyrus fragment. From that moment the magic name of Egypt and the reading of hieroglyphics became his destiny in life. It is said that he began to learn Greek, Arabic, Syriac and Coptic at the age of thirteen. Coptic, especially, proved vital for the decipherment of the hieroglyphs. Written in Greek letters, Coptic is the direct descendant of ancient Egyptian. Since it was the language of the ordinary people, it was used by the Christians in Egypt and remains to this day the liturgical language of the Egyptian Christians, the Copts.

Always, Champollion's thoughts reverted to the Rosetta Stone and to the ovals on it. Today we can distinguish the name of king or queen because it is surrounded by an oval line, a cord or knot to preserve the royal name from contact with common ones. The significance of the royal oval, or *cartouche,* had already been guessed by de Guignes and Zoëga in the late eighteenth century, but no one had guessed the meaning of the characters inside.

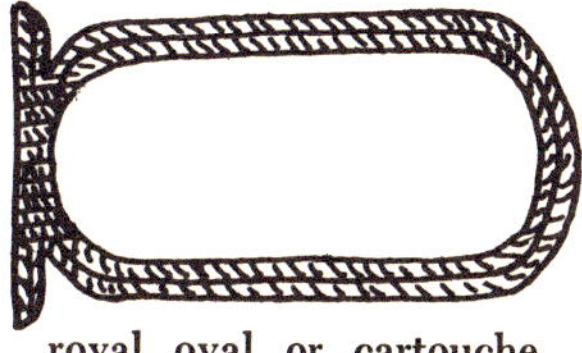
royal oval or cartouche

Champollion worked like a slave, but for a long time the solution eluded him. It occurred to him in September 1822 that the hieroglyphic pictures could, at least on occasion, be letters, and the moment he hit on the idea he found himself on the right track. From his study of the ovals he had already guessed that several of them contained the name Ptolemy, which appeared plainly enough in the Greek below.

With these clues he tackled the Ptolemy oval and finding a number of hieroglyphics approximately equivalent to the Greek letters, he read the name Ptolmess.

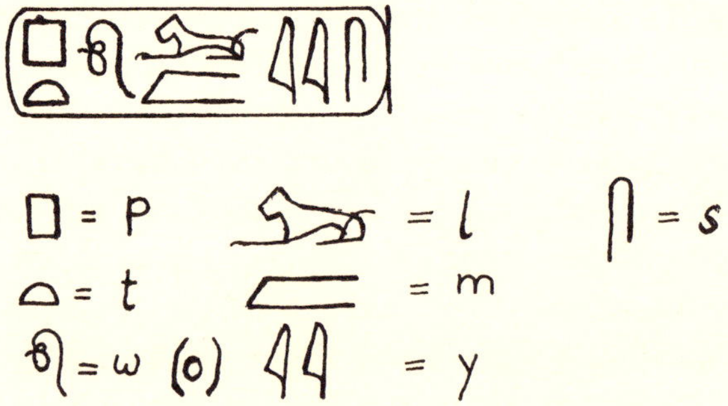

Cartouche of Ptolmess and its analysis

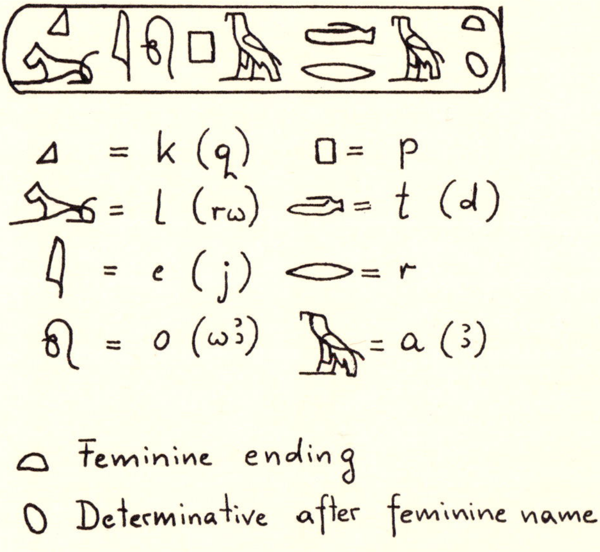

○ Feminine ending

O Determinative after feminine name

Cartouche of Cleopatra and its analysis

Still this was only a guess. Perhaps the puzzling hieroglyphic characters really meant something else. He must find some way of checking. Fortune favored him. An obelisk found on the island of Philae in the Nile had its inscription in two languages. It, too, had a Greek inscription at the bottom, hieroglyphs above. It, too, had royal ovals, or cartouches, of Ptolemy and another which he guessed to be that of Cleopatra, since in both occurred the hieroglyphic equivalents of the letters *p, o,* and *l* in just the position they should be. Besides, both names were written in Greek.

The obelisk was in effect a kind of second Rosetta Stone. It proved his first guess was correct. The two royal cartouches had furnished Champollion with a dozen different hieroglyphic letters and given him a tool for decipherment of other inscriptions.

Nothing now could deter Champollion. He collected all the cartouches he could find. Step by step he went through all the proper names, adding to his supply of known characters. The stones virtually began to speak. Ptolemy, Cleopatra and many others were addressing him genially from their ovals.

He used other inscriptions and monuments. At last he could read whole sentences. And then before his work was completely finished, he died. But Champollion had found the key for others to follow in his footsteps.

By now it may appear that the Egyptians had developed and were using a true alphabet. However, this is correct only to a limited degree, and primarily for the writing of foreign words or names. For such cases the Egyptians even invented a way of indicating vowels. For example, the Greek names of Ptolemy and Cleopatra contain indications of vowels; but the contemporary writing of Egyptian words still omitted them. Inside the cartouches there is one hieroglyph for each Greek letter, and in addition two more symbols which do not represent sounds. One is the common Egyptian feminine ending; the other, depicting an egg, indicates that the preceding group of signs are a woman's name.

From the Rosetta Stone it is easy to get the idea that all Egyptian writing was either the formal hieroglyphic or the flowing demotic, which more or less resembles the hasty, illegible handwriting of some of our friends. However, it was already known from the writers of antiquity that there had existed at least since the sixth century B.C. not two, but three forms of Egyptian writing. While the monumental hieroglyphs were the "carved holy signs" (this is what the word, in Greek, means), the demotic script was the script of the common folk (in Greek: *demos*) used for business and other everyday purposes at the time

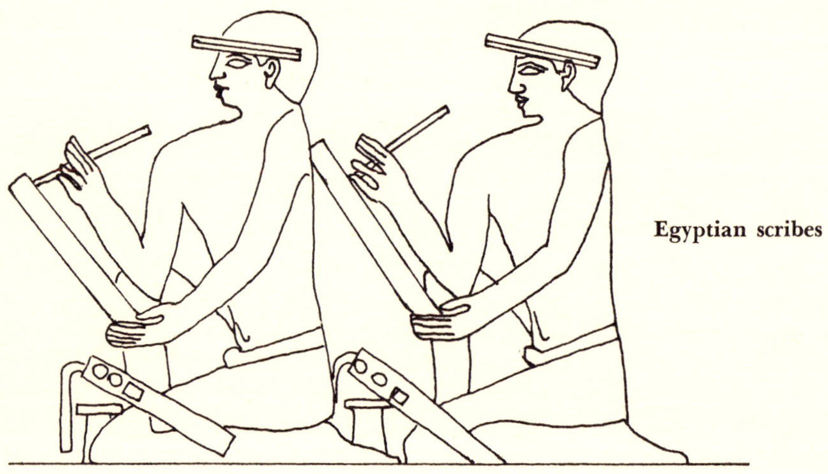

Egyptian scribes

when the Greeks came to Egypt. The third script was primarily used for religious books, for which reason the Greeks labelled it hieratic, meaning sacred. Like demotic, hieratic is written with pen and ink, as is illustrated by many a picture showing the scribes at work.

Its appearance reflects writing done with the easy flow of a pen, simplifying the complex hieroglyphs. Except for this simplification of form, hieratic as a system of writing is identical with hieroglyphs and is of the same antiquity. The difference between hieroglyphic and hieratic is the same as between modern handwriting and a monumental inscription on a public building.

Originally hieratic writing was used for anything written with pen and ink. However, as it became more and more simplified, the need arose for a formal script for writings of importance, such as religious books. This demand led to a separation of the secular and priestly writing in the late period, when hieratic was reserved for religious use, while the demotic, which had developed from it by further simplifications of the signs, was used for everyday script.

Note how the use of papyrus and reed pen simplified the old picture letters. In the most striking manner they show the effect of materials

Three kinds of script: Hieroglyphic (top); Hieratic (center); Demotic (bottom)

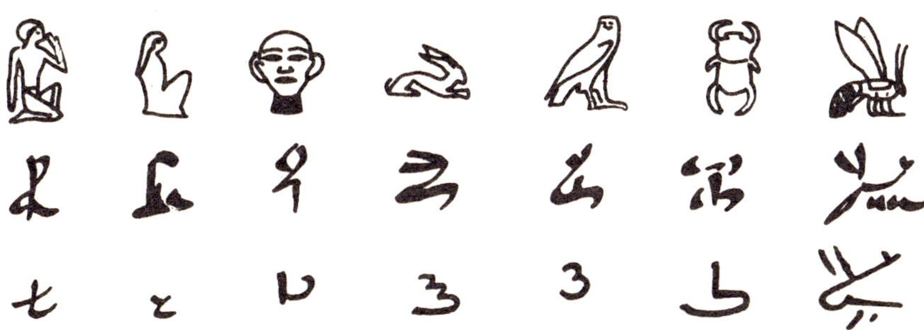

and tools on a people's way of writing. The same thing happened when the Mesopotamians wrote on clay. Try something other than paper and pen and see how your own writing will change.

Demotic has no place in the story of our form of writing, however, because it did not emerge until about 700 B.C. and that was centuries after the alphabet had been developed.

Although there existed, as we have seen, three different kinds of Egyptian scripts, hieroglyphic is the name by which Egyptian writing is known the world over. During all the centuries that hieratic was in use, the Egyptian clung to his fine old picturesque writing. On monument and tomb and temple he insisted on leaving his lordly, lovely hieroglyphs—perhaps the most picturesque form of writing ever made. Hence is it not with one script, with hieroglyphics alone, that the story of Egyptian writing should unfold?

Reading and writing were always considered a great art and were the profession of the scribes, a select class in society. Since at least 2000 B.C. schools existed in which the pupils were introduced to the art of writing in order to become officials. There are many admonitions to the young to take up the career of a scribe, considered the most advantageous when compared with other professions. It would free them from the hardship of physical labor and bring social status and an easy life.

Although we have one indication of a king writing a letter "with his own fingers," it is doubtful that this was common; the kings usually left such matters to their scribes and most probably could not read and write. Nevertheless we should not underestimate the extent of scribal education in ancient Egypt. Around 1500 B.C. the knowledge of writing was probably as widespread as it was in most of the Orient at the beginning of the twentieth century. Even in the village where the workmen lived who quarried the tombs for the kings, a school was established; and samples of their corrected homework show that the pupils there were not better or worse than in any rural school in the world.

When we look at the individual signs in a hieroglyphic inscription, we see a great many figures of people, animals and birds—sometimes a combination of them with human beings. The Sphinx, half man, half animal, is one example.

Animals and birds were closely associated with the Egyptian religion, and to the Egyptians religion meant much. And, as might be expected, the Egyptians also used other symbols for their hieroglyphic writing. Others depict plants, insects, beetles, weapons, objects of daily use, and geometrical figures. This wide array of recognizable signs makes it tempting to interpret the hieroglyphics as pictures. All approaches to the decipherment of hieroglyphs suffered from this tendency until Champollion's historic achievement.

To go back a moment: What really did happen in the evolution of the hieroglyphs? Like most people in the distant past, the inhabitants of the Nile valley tried to save memorable events from oblivion by finding some way to preserve them for eternity. To do this they tried to recreate the event by means of pictures of animals, objects, and scenes according to the impression those animals, objects, and scenes had made on them. By doing so they succeeded in telling the story of something that had happened or was desired. Such pictures could convey the image of man— but not his name. Simple pictures, as we know, are not always able to communicate the same message to everyone since they are likely to awake different associations in different persons. A picture of a lion might, for one spectator, produce a recollection of a particular beast seen or hunted; for another spectator, it might be the wish for a successful hunt; for a third, an evil which had harmed his flock. To depict a bull, a person would show a black, white or spotted one according to the particular specimen he had in mind, and another person might not know the same bull and thus not understand the particular message the artist had in mind.

There is a limit, however, to the complexity of the messages that pictures can convey, and in the development of picture-writing, as we have seen, one of the first stages is abstraction. Thus, for example, the artist might draw a simplified bovine animal which could stand for any cow or bull.

Concrete objects could be represented in this way, but not abstract ideas such as "honesty" or "sorrow." So the Egyptians, as did other peoples, evolved ideograms or idea-pictures. For example, our old friend "sorrow" or "weep" could be represented by an eye with tears; old age, by a man with a stick; writing, by a split reed and ink vial.

Further progress came when the Egyptians saw

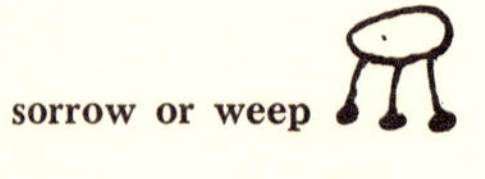

sorrow or weep

old man

writing

that there was a connection between the visual symbol which the scribe or artist drew and the spoken word for the same thing. The sounds made when pronouncing the word "bull" are as much a symbol for the animal as the simplified drawing. The difference is that one is heard, the other seen. Once the connection becomes clear, the written sign can be read aloud, and it ceases to be a picture of the creature, object or idea, and becomes a sign representing the spoken word.

To take an example, in Egyptian hieroglyphs the symbols shown represent a swallow and a beetle. This can be seen without any knowledge of the ancient Egyptian language. In that language, swallow is *wr* and beetle, *khpr*, pronounced with certain vowel sounds which are not known. An important step was taken when these two signs were used for other words which had the same pronunciation but different meaning: *wr* means both swallow and great; *khpr* means both beetle and become. By now the picture origins of the signs are of no importance; the signs stand for certain groups of sounds.

a swallow

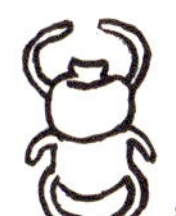

a beetle

Of course, the number of pairs of words which sound alike but have different meaning is limited. In English we have "there" and "their," etc. In Egyptian the same was true, so other means had to be devised for writing the remaining words. In so doing, the Egyptians stumbled on the principle of the alphabet. Words could be split up and written with separate signs for each consonant sound.

This may have been suggested by the existence of several words consisting of one consonant sound

strip of cloth

snake

lake

and a following vowel, which is now no longer known. For example, a strip of cloth is *s* (followed by an unknown vowel); similarly, the word for snake is *dj* (as in *j*ust); and lake is *sh* (as in *sh*ine). By using these signs for the sounds with which one said the words, the Egyptians had the basis of an alphabet.

But there were not enough words of one syllable for all the consonantal sounds of the language, so to fill in what was lacking they resorted to a method which we call *acrophony*. Acrophony means the indication of a sound by the use of a picture or name of something which begins with the sound wanted. We still use this method for spelling out names over the telephone: "Paul. *p,* for Peter; *a,* for Albert; *u,* for under; *l,* as in Leo." To illustrate how acrophony was used to develop sound signs, a few are given below.

With the help of acrophony the Egyptians built a store of twenty-four signs, each of which signified one particular sound. In use, these signs have the character of letters, and since they include all the consonants of the Egyptian language one might consider them a kind of alphabet.

A FEW LETTERS DEVELOPED BY THE USE OF ACROPHONY

OBJECT	PICTURE SIGN	NAME	SOUND VALUE
mouth		ro	r
hill		qa'	q
hand		deret	d

THE EGYPTIAN "ALPHABET"

SOUND VALUE	SIGN	SOUND VALUE	SIGN
'		kh	
y			
'		s	
w			
b		sh	
p		q	
f		k	
m		g	
n		t	
r		th	
h		d	
ḥ		dj	

No doubt some readers may compare the signs in this "alphabet" with signs in the Ptolemy and Cleopatra cartouches and find that some of them may differ for the same letter. This is not strange when one considers that the ancient writing shows two kinds of *k* and no less than four kinds of *t* and *d*. It would appear that the scribes never got around to spelling the same way at all times. In one inscription there have been found ten variations in the spelling of one word.

As much as it might look like an alphabet, the system nevertheless cannot be considered to be a complete alphabet. For one thing, there was no established order of the signs. Secondly, they indicate only consonants, and not the vowels. Like most of the Semitic writing systems, Egyptian never had vowels. For readers accustomed to this system there was no difficulty in providing the vowels according to context.

Once signs had been adopted to represent each consonantal sound in writing, it could have been possible for the ancient Egyptians to write every word with only twenty-four signs, just as we do with twenty-six letters. But this final step was never taken. As a result the Egyptians were burdened by over three thousand hieroglyphic signs, at least three to four hundred of which were in constant use and were the minimum requirement for any reading.

Thus the Egyptians used picture-symbols representing sounds, whether the sounds meant the thing shown by the picture-symbol or something else. For words which could still not be expressed by this system, the so-called alphabet was used to fill in.

But the Egyptians never progressed so far as to trust their "letters." They continued to look upon a word as an idea and the writing of a message as giving a picture or image. So they developed a series of signs expressing a host of basic ideas, and, after writing the words in the manner described, they added another symbol which was written but not spoken.

This sign was a picture expressing a basic idea. For example. after words expressing all forms of movement such as walking, running, or jumping, a symbol representing a pair of walking legs was used; everything that flew, including locusts, had a bird symbol accompanying it.

walking legs

These determinatives explain the meaning of the written word. Thus when the word *sf* meant 'yesterday,' a picture of the sun was added. When it meant 'child,' it was followed by the symbol of a child.

yesterday

child

In addition to indicating the general category within which a particular word fell, there were other uses for these determinatives. They could, for example, give a more precise meaning to the word. Thus the word to travel, *nmj,* could have either of two determinatives, the first referring to travel on foot, the second to travel by boat.

travel on foot

travel by boat

We should not forget, however, that the hiero-glyphs were the product of the Egyptians and best suited to their needs. But when the Egyptians tried to write foreign words they had difficulties. During the middle of the second millenium they came in close contact with other peoples and were forced to develop techniques of writing foreign words which did not conform to the pattern of the Egyptian language. For this task they started from their own system of writing but used only those signs which indicated one sound. They even found ways of expressing vowels, and with twenty-four signs they had a real alphabet at hand with which they could write any word, be it Cretan, Nubian or Semitic. But though they had the tool, they never used it for their own language.

Due to the strong cultural influence of Egypt in the Near East and in particular in Palestine, which

A FEW DETERMINATIVES

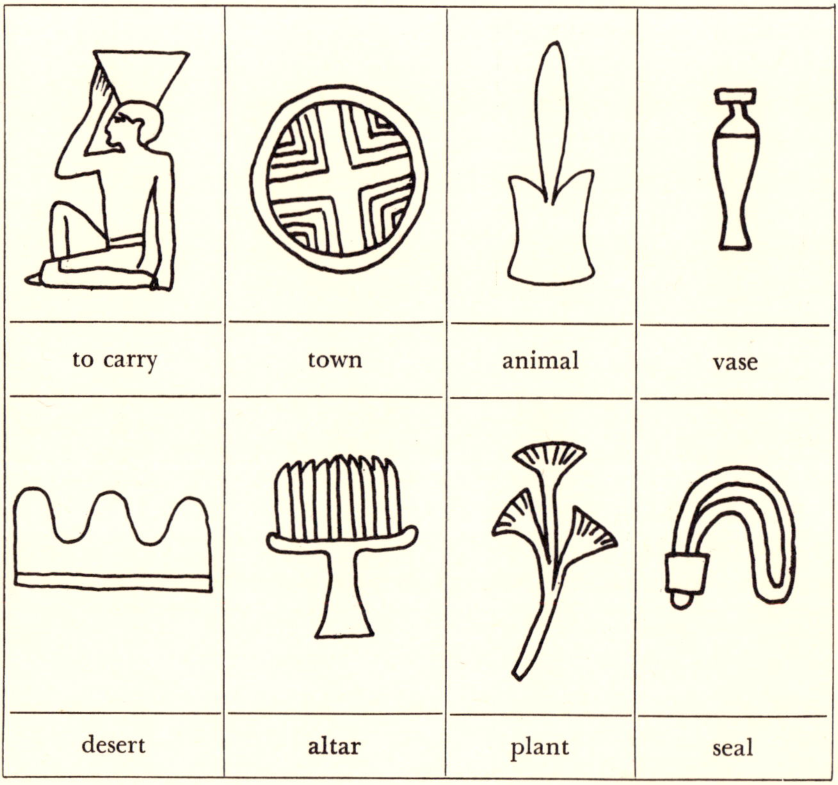

to carry	town	animal	vase
desert	altar	plant	seal

for five hundred years was politically under Egyptian control, this system developed by the Egyptians was adopted by the Semites, who had up to this time developed no writing of their own. This adopted form ultimately became the basis for all later alphabetic writing. Thus ultimately our writing goes back, although through many transformations, to the enigmatic hieroglyphs.

CHAPTER EIGHT

The Phoenicians

Since the Egyptians did not arrive at a true alphabet, who were the first to have one? To guide us in our search we have a very good clue in the word alphabet, which is nothing more than the names of the first two letters, *alpha* and *beta*, in the Greek alphabet. Following up that clue we find that many of the Greek letters had names —such as *alpha, beta, gamma, delta,* and so on— which are strikingly similar to the names *'āleph, bēth, gamel, dāleth* and so on, of Semitic letters.

Hence it is not surprising that credit for making that last step toward a writing system without use of pictographs, ideograms, determinatives and syllables should be given to the Semites; nor that

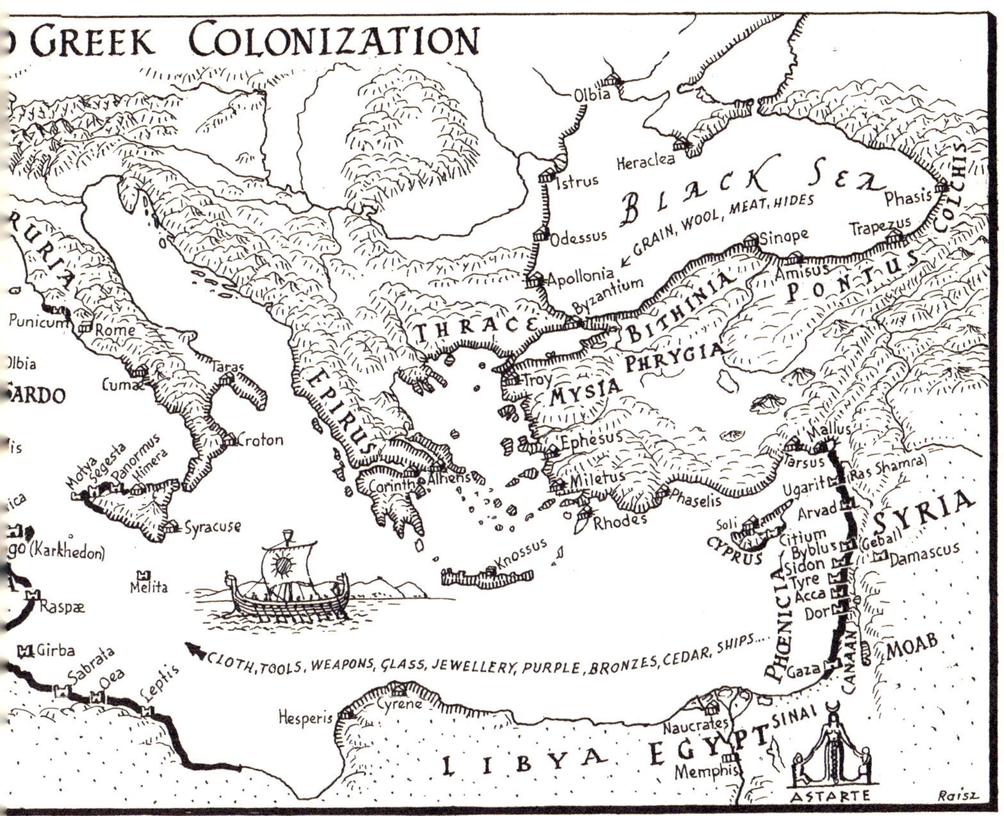

the Semites, for this achievement, simple as it
seems to us, should be ranked among the greatest
benefactors of mankind.

Now we must remember that the term "Semites" does not refer to a particular group but
to many peoples speaking Semitic languages. For
instance, the speech of the Hebrews and Moabites
was as much like the Phoenician as Scottish is like
English or Danish like Norwegian.

A globe of the ancient world will show that the
Semites occupied an exceedingly small part of the
ancient world. Small it is true, but what an important part. Living as they did on the land
bridge between Mesopotamia and Egypt, they

were influenced by both civilizations. Indeed, the two factors of geography and culture contributed greatly to their invention of the alphabet.

The narrow Phoenician coastal strip was the land route between Asia and Africa; its shore was one terminus of the sea lanes that connected Europe with Asia and Africa. The most important trade routes for merchants and caravans of the ancient world passed through it. It was the crossroads of civilization, a great meeting place of many peoples where a lively intermingling of cultures took place. The Phoenicians borrowed from all of them.

In that small part of the Old World lived some of the most celebrated peoples in history—the Amorites and Aramaeans, the Hebrews and Phoenicians and others who make up a stirring roll call of the names of antiquity.

Now which one of these Semitic peoples should be given the credit for making that last step toward alphabetic writing? With such a wide choice it might seem that we should proceed with considerable caution before coming to any conclusion. Fortunately for us that particular problem was settled long ago. Scholars agree and the accumulated evidence is convincing that, at some time, the inhabitants of various parts of the Greek world acquired the alphabet through contacts with the seafaring Phoenicians who were part of the group of northwest Semitic peoples called the Canaanites, made up of Moabites, Hebrews, Phoenicians and others. From our point of view, therefore, the most important of the Semitic alphabets was the Phoenician, because from it came the Greek and hence the European forms.

For many of us the Phoenicians are merely a part of Roman history. We immediately think of Carthage and Hannibal's march over the Alps, but our interest in them goes back hundreds of years before the Punic Wars. So let us take a look at these Phoenicians whose ships sailed many seas and whose merchants bargained in many ports.

If you confuse the Phoenicians with the Canaanites that would not be surprising, for they called themselves Canaanites and their land Canaan. And they did, in fact, belong to the Canaanite peoples in the sense of the biblical term. Later the Greeks began calling them Phoenicians from the Greek word "phoenix," which means purple, for these particular Canaanites had acquired great fame as dyemakers, especially of royal purple, which they extracted from a certain shellfish.

The Phoenicians (historians now use the Greek name to identify these ancient Canaanites) lived on the coastal part of the country which we now call Syria. Along the Syrian seaboard great cities grew and became famous as seaports and marts of trade: Ugarit, the most northerly; Gebal, called Byblos by the Greeks, after their word for papyrus reed and book from which comes our word Bible; Sidon, for long the most important Phoenician city; and Tyre, mistress of the seas. For centuries Tyre was invulnerable, being built on an island in the sea. Though often attacked by mighty enemies, Tyre carried on business as usual. Now the harbor is filled with silt and not one stone of ancient Tyre remains upon another.

On a globe of the ancient world Phoenicia is only a tiny spot on the earth's surface, a narrow strip of rocky land along the coast. Small wonder then that the Phoenicians developed a strongly un-Semitic love for the sea or that they found the sea more friendly than their land and turned more and more to foreign commerce and became the greatest mariners of their time.

From the mountain slopes they cut down trees to fashion galleys, propelled by one rectangular sail and slaves at double banks of oars. With no compass to guide him, only dire necessity would cause a sea captain to sail out of sight of land or venture out at night. But gradually their knowledge of navigation, of currents and winds, developed to the point where bold Phoenician pilots sailed the ocean waters.

Their vessels, some over one hundred feet long, plied the trade routes that linked Egypt, Babylonia and the Near East with Italy, Greece and Spain. At strategic points along the Mediterranean they established trading posts which grew into prosperous cities such as Carthage.

They trafficked in everything, even in people, and their wealth increased. They spread around the Mediterranean the wares of others and the merchandise they themselves manufactured.

From the standpoint of the Phoenicians their trade and industry was their most important work. From our standpoint they did one thing of far more lasting value. For this achievement alone, they deserve a niche in the hall of civilized nations. Among the wares they carried abroad was the greatest article of export of any kind, of any age—the first alphabet. This brings us to the critical question: How and when did the Phoenician alphabet come into being? Scholars have long been groping for the answer. Theories, which were thought to have been settled once and for all, have repeatedly been upset by some new discovery. And who knows but that tomorrow some other new find may upset all present ideas?

Did some brilliantly inspired Phoenician just make up an alphabet? Since such an answer is far too easy, then where are the ancestors of the twenty-two Phoenician letters to be found?

A French scholar tried to prove that each Phoenician letter came from a corresponding Egyptian character. An Englishman advanced the suggestion that Cretan characters lay behind the Phoenician alphabet. Another has proved to his satisfaction that parts of the Phoenician alphabet were borrowed from the Babylonians. Meanwhile other scholars have not been idle—each country of the Eastern Mediterranean has been seriously regarded as a legitimate ancestor.

Thus we see that many scholars feel that the Phoenicians leaned heavily on the writing of other peoples, but they are unable to agree on *which* people. One might think that each new discovery should have helped to clarify the problem, yet they seem only to add to the conflicts already existing over this most controversial period in the story of writing.

How easy our task would be if each Phoenician letter could be traced back to its source! The plain fact is that this cannot be done with any hope of agreement. So there we are, still lost in a jungle of theories and no nearer to a solution of that critical question, "How and when did the Phoenician alphabet come into being?"

Let us try another approach. We need important discoveries to serve as guideposts for a reasonable answer to that question: discoveries of inscriptions from 2000 to 800 B.C., which play a vital role in the history of the development of alphabetic writing. The sites of these important discoveries are all located in the area of Sinai, Palestine and Syria, a part of the ancient world occupied by Semitic-speaking peoples.

About 2000 B.C.   Byblos Script

At Byblos (Gebal of the Old Testament) a pseudo-hieroglyphic script in a hitherto unknown kind of writing was discovered in 1923. It looked something like Egyptian but was not. Scholars thought that this script must be syllabic. It had not reached the stage of alphabetic writing. It probably showed Egyptian influences, and also showed that one or more attempts to create a new system of writing were made in Phoenicia at an early date.

About 1800-1500 B.C.   Sinaitic Inscriptions

On the Sinai Peninsula inscriptions written in a Semitic language were found in 1905. This system of writing consists of twenty to thirty different signs. While some words can be read, the decipherment is not yet finished. Some scholars regard this as the earliest alphabetic writing.

About 1600 B.C.(?) Canaanite Inscriptions

Inscriptions have been found in Palestine, written in what is termed for convenience the early Canaanite script. They are not yet deciphered, though several attempts have been made. According to some eminent scholars the script constitutes an important "missing link" in the history of our alphabet because it represents the long-sought intermediate stage between the Sinaitic and earliest Phoenician scripts. Others think it is earlier than the inscriptions from Sinai.

1400 B.C. Ugarit Alphabet

At Ras Shamra, the site of ancient Ugarit, a large number of clay tablets were found in 1929. The real surprise at Ras Shamra was the discovery that the Phoenicians of ancient Ugarit had compiled a simple alphabet that used cuneiform signs and one little tablet, only 2 inches by ½ inch, has inscribed on it the thirty signs in the

Ugarit clay tablet

Courtesy of the National Museum of Damascus

Semitic order—the first complete "A B C." It was a purely alphabetic system with no ideograms and no determinatives.

This alphabet, however, had no connection with the cuneiform system of writing except that the signs were impressed in a similar way with a stylus on clay. Evidently the scribes of Ugarit had adapted the cuneiform wedge-shaped marks to their own simple Phoenician alphabet so they could write on clay.

Sound	ʻ	h	z	s	ʻ	Sh
Phoenician Letter	1	∃	I	‡	o	w
Cuneiform Letter	Y	⊨	⸙	⸙	∆	⸙

Ugarit Signs resembling Phoenician Letters

(after Diringer)

About 1000 B.C.   Ahiram Epitaph

Even more exciting than the Byblos pseudo-hieroglyphic script, there was also found at Byblos in 1923 an epitaph on the sarcophagus of a Phoenician king of Byblos named Ahiram (Akhiram).

This is the earliest example of an inscription of more than a few words in the fully developed

Phoenician alphabet. It is in a mature state and gives the impression that the alphabet had been in use for some time.

$$\langle 9 7 \cup L \} \cdot \} 9 \boxplus \mathsf{K} \} 9 \cdot L 0 9 + \mathsf{K}$$

'tb°l : bn 'ḥrm : mlk gbl

'Ittoba°l bin 'Aḥiram milk Gubl

Ittoba°l, son of Aḥiram, king of Gubl (Byblos)

THE ROMANCE OF WRITING by *K. G. Irwin*

The Ahiram epitaph

850 B.C. Moabite or Mesha Stone

The inscription on the Moabite Stone is the record made by Mesha, King of Moab, of his rebellion against Jehoram, King of Israel and, therefore, is the oldest inscription whose date can be fixed by the contents. It was found in 1868 and was often thought to be the earliest inscription in alphabetic writing until the discovery of the Ahiram Epitaph.

Here our interest in Palestinian archeology ceases because the Greeks borrowed the alphabet from the Phoenicians about one hundred years after the date of the Moabite Stone.

The exact dating of all these writings, including the Greek, is impossible since this question of dating is still under discussion among scholars. Indeed it would be possible without much difficulty to write a whole book on the subject. Even so certain facts do emerge from the guide posts. It is evident that the evolution of alphabetic writing extended over a long period of time and that a number of different attempts were being made

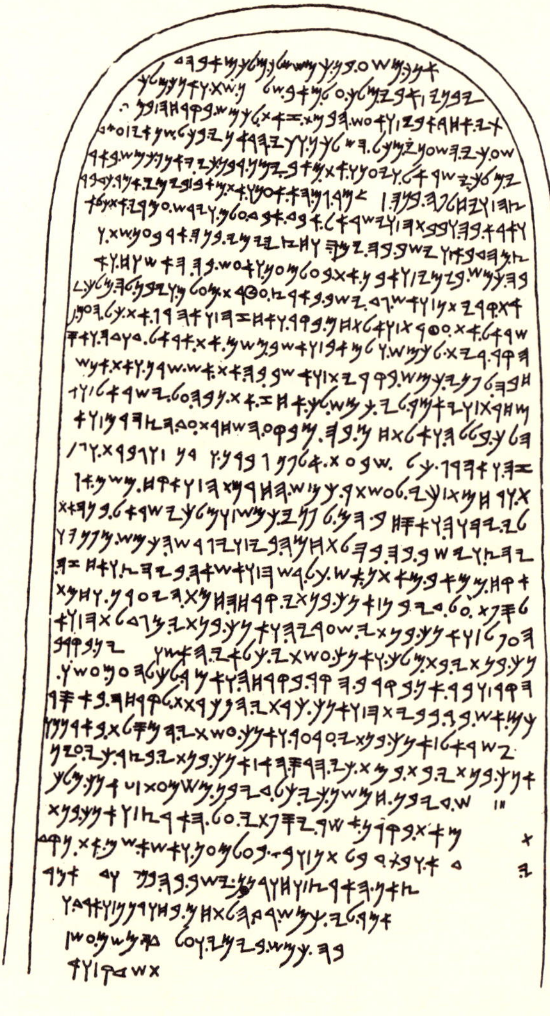

Stele of Mesha, King of Moab

by Semitic peoples to form new scripts. We may say that among the Semites alphabet-making was in the air during the second millenium B.C.

Although alphabetic writing may seem quite simple to us, in the ancient world its invention came very slowly. Presumably it was invented by Semites, since it is at first the alphabet of the Canaanites alone. It was not used by the Babylonians or Egyptians, so we can only conclude that somewhere among the Semites of Palestine and Syria this great invention took place, and rapidly it spread to all the peoples of that area—the Hebrews, the Moabites, the Phoenicians and so on.

The guide posts show that the Phoenician alphabet developed from the earlier Canaanite scripts, but they do not tell us which system of writing gave the idea and provided the basis on which the Canaanites built.

A Babylonian origin may sound plausible to some scholars, for Babylonian was the official dipplomatic language of the ancient world, the ancient Oriental "French" of the second millenium. The Tel-el-Amarna letters, written in the language and cuneiform script of Babylonia, were the official correspondence from rulers in Phoenicia and other places to the Pharaohs of Egypt. Furthermore, the fact that the Ugarit alphabet was written in cuneiform-type marks on clay tablets testifies to the influence which the Babylonian civilization had upon the Phoenicians of ancient Ugarit.

As has been mentioned before, a few have claimed that the Cretans should be given more credit. Nor should we disregard the influence of mighty nations like the Hittites upon the Semitic Phoenicians. Suffice it to say that the centuries allowed ample opportunity for other systems of writing—Cretan, Hittite, Babylonian, and Assyrian—to contribute whatever they had to offer. And the Phoenicians were a practical people. They took something from everybody and no doubt borrowed ideas from others for their alphabet.

Therefore, to repeat, attempts have been made to prove that the alphabet was derived from cuneiform, from Cretan and other sources but none of these has found wide acceptance.

Of all the ancient cultures none remains to be considered here except the Egyptian. Now take a look at Egypt. For one thing, the giant of the Nile was the first great power to stretch out its tentacles for trade with the North Semitic group of nations of which Phoenicia was one. Egypt's influence in the Tyro-Palestine coastal strip was dominant from about 2000 to 1200 B.C. while the Semitic alphabet was being developed. In the seaports of Ugarit and Tyre the Pharaohs had their consuls. Byblos had close trade relations with Egypt. Important, one may say, but not convincing, because other nations also exercised great influence on these Semites. We need more than evidence of the mere exercise of influence upon the Phoenicians to provide a convincing argument in favor of any one people.

There are several fundamental arguments in favor of the Nile people. The writing techniques of other mighty peoples had reached an advanced stage but could not get beyond the syllabic. On the other hand, as you will recall, the Egyptians had produced not only something close to an alphabetic system for writing their own language but also a fairly simple way to write foreign words.

Because of the strong political and cultural influence of Egypt in Syro-Palestine, it would have been only natural if the Semites in this region had just taken over the writing of their masters. However, the story is not that simple.

We should keep in mind that the Egyptian writing system was geared to the Egyptian language. This is true in particular for the twenty-four letters they used to indicate single consonants and which formed a kind of alphabet. Some of these letters had been developed by acrophony. Its principle, as you will recall, means indicating a sound by using a picture or name of something which begins with the sound you want: B for Baker and so on. In this way the Egyptians used some of their hieroglyphs not to indicate a whole word but its initial sound, and thus the hieroglyph became a letter sound; for example, *ro* (the Egyptian word for mouth) became the letter *r*.

Once some Semite had learned the revolutionary advantages to be derived from acrophony, it would seem a natural thing for him to take over the hieroglyphics along with the acrophonic principle. However, the Egyptians and the Semites in Syro-Palestine, needless to say, did not have the same name for any object. For example, note how the Egyptian *n* and *r* changed to the Semitic *m* and *p* respectively.

So what happened? As far as the Semites were familiar with the Egyptian script, they knew it chiefly in the cursive form, the so-called hieratic. Not knowing what objects the hieratic signs actually depicted, they gave names to the signs after the objects they recognized in them. The Egyptian sign used to indicate the consonant *d* reminded them of a door leaf. Thus they called it *dāleth,* "door," and used it to indicate *d*. In this same way the hieratic form of the sign depicting a shouting man was interpreted as an oxhead, called *'āleph.*

Using this principle of acrophony, the Semites connected each letter with an object that had the sound of that letter at the beginning of the name. Some of these objects were taken over from the lordly hieroglyphic but chiefly from its simplified form, the hieratic.

From this bare outline of the way the Semitic letters came into being it would seem reasonable to assume that the only ancient system of writing which could have influenced the invention of the Semitic alphabet is the Egyptian. In fact, what other people have so strong a claim?

Although we do not know definitely where the

Egyptian				Semitic				
Hieroglyph	Meaning	Name	Letter	Object	Meaning	Name	Symbol	Letter
〰	Waters	Unknown	N	〰	Waters	Mem		M
◠	Mouth	Ro	R	◠	Mouth	Peh		P

great invention of the alphabet was made, some scholars think it was on the Sinai Peninsula which borders on Egypt. We know that on the Sinai Peninsula the Pharaohs had vast operations for the mining of copper and turquoise. The mines were worked by crews of local Semitic natives under the direction of Egyptian officials. Under such circumstances one may easily suppose that some Egyptian scribes "taught" intelligent native foremen the rudiments of writing to save them the labor of keeping simple records. Also we may suppose that a few of the natives were intelligent enough to grasp the acrophonic principle and to discover the advantage of using a few characters instead of the innumerable characters used by their masters for their lordly hieroglyphics.

At any rate, the system of writing which these

A FEW OF THE LETTERS DEVELOPED BY ACROPHONY FROM THE HIERATIC

EGYPTIAN			SEMITIC			
Hieroglyph	*Hieratic*	*Meaning*	*Meaning*	*Name*	*Letter*	*Sign*
		shouting man	ox	'aleph	'	
		hand	door	dāleth	d	
		arms	palm of hand	kaph	k	
		lion	ox goad	lāmedh	l	

Semites in Sinai developed was a bare skeleton of some two dozen consonantal signs. This is important, for the fewer different signs there are in a script, the greater the chance of its being alphabetic.

Unfortunately, these Sinaitic inscriptions are all quite short and very few identical groups of characters (that is, identical words) recur. But there is one group of four characters which recurs several times and these have been identified as *B^{c}lt,* spelling the name of the primitive Semitic goddess, *Ba^{c}alat:*

In these ancient Semitic writings, we can recognize the sign for *lāmedh* (ox-goad), or *l;* and for *tāw* (mark), the letter *t.* There also appear in the Sinai inscriptions several signs, familiar to us by now, such as the wavy line for *m.*

Even if this theory is wrong and the alphabet was invented by some other people in another place, the process of using the Egyptian signs as a basis must have been the same, so it may not be wrong to quote the example of Sinai. Either here in this way, or nearby in a similar way, the true alphabet was for the first and last time invented.

This Semitic alphabet divided into two branches not long after its invention: a South Semitic branch used by the Arabs, and a North Semitic branch used by the Hebrews and Phoenicians. Since the Phoenician is the ancestor of our alphabet, we shall follow only the history of this one.

Writing, as we have seen, went through various stages of improvement, as it passed from Egypt to the Semites until it was perfected, but that was not done all at once.

PHOENICIAN ALPHABET

SOUND VALUE	SIGN	NAME	MEANING
'		'āleph	ox
b		bēth	house
g		gīmel	throw-stick
d		dāleth	door
h		hē'	(unknown)
w		wāw	hook
z		zayin	weapon (?)
ḥ		ḥēth	fence
ṭ		ṭēth	(unknown)
y		yōdh	hand
k		kaph	palm of hand
l		lāmedh	ox-goad
m		mēm	water
n		nūn	fish
s		sāmekh	support
'		'ayin	eye
p		pēh	mouth
ṣ		ṣadhē	fishhook
q		qōph	monkey
r		rēsh	head
sh		shīn	tooth
t		tāw	mark

GREECE
100 miles
ADRIATIC SEA
BLACK SEA
GRECIA MAGNA
Tarent
Apollonia
EPIRUS
MACEDONIA
THRACE
Byzantium
Kalkhedon
Thasos
Olympus
Sybaris
IONIAN SEA
Croton
Kerkyra
Pelas
THESSALY
Abydos
Dardanelles
Troy
PHRYGIA
(until 700 B.C.
AEGEAN SEA
LYDIA
Phocæa
Sardes
Delphi
BŒOTIA
Khalkis
Thebes
ATTICA
Corinth
Athens
ARCADIA
Mycæne
Tiryns
Olympia
Sparta
LACONIA
Pylos
Smyrna
Kolophon
Ephesos
Miletos
CARIA
Delos
Ionian
Kythera
Knossos
Dorians
Rhodes
CRETE
Itanos
Raisz

CHAPTER NINE

The Greeks

We are now ready for the Greek story. But we shall not start it with tales of gods, demi-gods and heroes as the Greeks themselves might have done. Nor shall we start it with the age of Pericles when the Parthenon rose in all its glory; nor with Socrates or Plato, his greatest pupil, for the alphabet took roots in Greece long before they were born.

The Greek-speaking peoples had not always lived in Hellas, as they called the Greek Peninsula. Little is known about their cradle land. In the early dawn of history they appear to have been a wild, semi-barbarous people who lived in the mountainous region to the north—perhaps in the Balkans, for Greece proper forms an outward extension of the Balkan Mountains.

The Greeks were European. Their Indo-European type of language was quite different from the Semitic languages in which the consonants express the basic meaning of the words. And their language, as was the case with the Phoenicians, proved to be an important factor in the development of their alphabet.

Greek tradition tells us of two main waves of invading Greeks which swept down upon the pre-Hellenic civilization that had flourished in Crete, on the Aegean islands and in the major cities on the mainland of Greece.

The first wave seems to have been the Achaeans, who gradually established themselves in many parts of Greece, in Mycenae and Pylos and other mainland cities. As might be expected, the pace of Greek development was speeded by contact with the nearby island of Crete. Indeed, the earliest roots of Greek culture appear to have grown on Crete, which rivaled the civilizations of Egypt and Mesopotamia. And thus began the first major civilization of Europe.

In time, as we have seen in a former chapter, the balance of power shifted from ancient Crete to the Greek mainland, and the Mycenaeans became undisputed masters of the Aegean world. They learned seamanship from the Cretans. For a time they dominated the sea lanes of the Mediterranean.

No Grecian city is more legend-haunted than Mycenae, the city of Agamemnon and other famous names. These were the men and times immortalized by Homer.

Then, as in later times, Greece was split by its many natural barriers into a number of city-states. In no sense was she a united nation, such as our own. Greece was merely a patchwork of small kingdoms, most of them very small. They were constantly fighting and bickering among themselves.

The city-states depended for their livelihood upon widespread foreign trade, and some historians suggest that the Greeks besieged Troy not over Helen but to free their trade routes to the Black Sea from the Trojans. When their trade routes were gradually severed by constant raids, disaster was inevitable. Those cities which were not wiped out slowly withered. It is believed that Mycenae weakened economically before being destroyed.

The decline of Mycenaean civilization was either caused by or accompanied by the second wave of invading Greeks. The Dorians, a backward and illiterate people, moved down through central Greece and the islands, perhaps themselves being pushed by upheavals in the vast barbarian hinterland. They infiltrated the stricken land, bringing new chaos to an already prostrate civilization. The Mycenaean world crumbled. The so-called dark age of Greece ensued.

Out of the troubled darkness came the wonderful achievement of the Greek alphabet. It is that achievement, and how it came about, in which we are interested.

The Phoenicians, as we know, became a maritime nation because their narrow coastline was hemmed in by mountains. Likewise the Greeks were forced to take to the sea because of the mountainous character of their country. Hence it should not be surprising if foreign commerce caused the two to clash, for trade and commerce have been the prime causes of war for thousands of years. At any rate it would seem that the Phoenicians, in their active exploitation of the Mediterranean region, were in contact with the Greek-speaking peoples for an indefinitely long time, and that each must have taken advantage of what the other had to offer.

According to Greek tradition, the Greeks learned the art of writing from the Phoenicians, and serious scholars are in agreement with that tradition. The oldest forms of the Greek letters from alpha to tau are virtually identical with the most ancient Semitic characters. The chief alteration came later when the direction of writing became left to right and B, for instance, was reversed. The order of the Greek letters corresponds, with few exceptions, to the order of the Semitic letters. Also the Greek names for their letters demonstrate their Semitic origin. Here are a few of these lettters and their names:

LETTER	A	B	D	Z	K	L	M	N	R	T
SEMITIC NAME	*'āleph*	*bēth*	*dāleth*	*zayin*	*kaph*	*lāmedh*	*mēm*	*nūn*	*rēsh*	*tāw*
GREEK NAME	*alpha*	*beta*	*delta*	*zeta*	*kappa*	*lambda*	*mu*	*nu*	*rho*	*tau*

Whereas the Greek names of letters are meaningless in Greek, the Semitic ones are words in the Semitic languages. To the Greeks, ox was *bous,* not *'āleph* or *alpha.* A house was *oikia,* not *bēth* or *beta.* The Greeks, when they borrowed their alphabet from the Semitic Phoenicians, took the names along with the letters to which they belonged.

It is also evident that the Greeks took over the acrophonic principle which, as we know, the Semites borrowed from the Egyptians. That is, the initial sound of a foreign word, which the Greeks had to repeat, became the sound of the letter that the sign represented. Thus the meaningless word *bēth,* which the Greeks knew as *beta,* became the name of the letter B, and so on.

Greek tradition gives Kadmos of Thebes the credit for bringing the alphabet to Greece. Whether or not Kadmos was just a legendary hero and credit belongs to someone else makes little difference. At least we know that someone did bring the Phoenician alphabet to Greece and a reasonable theory seems to be that credit should be given to Greek traders who established a settlement on the Syro-Phoenician coast and learned the twenty-two letters of the Phoenician alphabet.

But even with the alphabet safely on Greek soil, the task of adjusting the Phoenician way of writing to Greek uses was no easy matter. For one thing, the Phoenicians wrote entirely with consonants; the Greeks needed vowel sounds for their Indo-European language.

To the Phoenicians, all of their twenty-two letters were easy to pronounce. But to the ancient Greeks, only those letter names which began with consonant sounds familiar to the Greeks were easy to pronounce; a few were fairly difficult; the rest, impossible.

Letters which express sounds common to the Semitic and Greek languages and which also demonstrate the acrophonic principle are shown on page 116. They were easy for the Greeks to handle and were taken over without change except, as might be expected, the Semitic names end with a consonant while the Greek names end with a vowel.

Other Semitic letters were adopted for slightly different Greek sounds; for instance, the letter *ṭēth,* which represented the hard Semitic *t,* was adapted for the Greek *th.* The Greeks also added certain letters for sounds not expressed by any of the Semitic letters.

Some of the letters in our alphabet were not present because the Greek tongue did not require them, and some were used with different sound values, such as their *h (eta). Eta* was h at first but was put to a new use as *ē* in the Ionic alphabet, which eventually became the alphabet of Greece in general.

As we know, the forms of the letters were fluid, so to speak, and they changed as they spread from country to country. On the whole, however, there is a remarkable degree of similarity between the Phoenician and early Greek letters, although in various Greek local alphabets the letter signs have been reversed, elaborated, simplified, or even stood on end. In fact, they have suffered all the unintentional treatment likely to befall a meaningless shape with an unintelligible name.

With so many local variations in the letter shapes it should not be surprising that there is no general agreement on the correct shape for every early Greek letter. The following chart, however,

ALPHABETS — PHOENICIAN TO GREEK

PHOENICIAN			GREEK		
Sound Value	*Name*	*Sign*	*Sound Value*	*Name*	*Sign*
'	'āleph		a	alpha	
b	bēth		b	beta	
g	gīmel		g	gamma	
d	dāleth		d	delta	
h	hē'		e	epsilon	
w	wāw		w	(digamma)	
z	zayin		dz	zeta	
ḥ	ḥēth		h	eta	
ṭ	ṭēth		th	theta	
y	yōdh		i	iota	
k	kaph		k	kappa	
l	lāmedh		l	lambda	
m	mēm		m	mu	
n	nūn		n	nu	
s	sāmekh		x	xi	
'	'ayin		o	omikron	
p	pēh		p	pi	
ṣ	ṣadhē		s	san	
q	qōph		q	koppa	
r	rēsh		r	rho	
sh	shīn		s	sigma	
t	tāw		t	tau	
			u	upsilon	
			ph	phi	
			ch	chi	

is sufficiently accurate to give a comparison between the Phoenician and early Greek letters.

The greatest contribution of the Greeks was the addition of vowels to the alphabet. The Semites, as we know, had no signs for vowels and the reader had to supply the vowel which suited the context. But vowels played a prominent role in Greek, so it was essential that the Greek alphabet should have them.

This the Greeks did by using Semitic letters which represented sounds which were unknown to Greek. What the Greeks did, then, was to convert seemingly unnecessary consonant signs into vowels, and to express the vowels by signs on an equal footing with the consonants.

In taking over the Semitic names of letters, the Greeks naturally had difficulty with the pronunciation of some. Thus the very first Semitic letter, *'āleph,* was not needed as a consonant because Greek was not so rich in gutturals as the Semitic. In pronouncing the name, the Greeks ignored the initial guttural sound, so the name to the Greek ear began with the second sound *a* and, in accordance with the acrophonic principle, was used for the vowel sound *a*. In this way the Semitic *'āleph* became the Greek *alpha.*

Similarly, the Semitic *hē* lost its initial consonant sound when pronounced by the Greeks and took the value of the vowel sound which followed it, namely, *e (epsilon). Epsilon* was used for the short and long *e* in the Western Greek alphabet. In other Greek alphabets, however, *epsilon* was used for the short *e* and *ḥēth* became *eta* for use as the long *e.*

Nor did the Greeks need the Semitic *yōdh* as a

consonantal sign since they had no consonantal *y*. In their pronunciation of the name of this letter, they substituted a vowel *i (iota)* for the consonant *y* and used the character as a sign for the vowel *i*.

iota

The sign for the vowel *o* developed from the former Semitic *'ayin,* in which the initial consonant was lost when the name was pronounced by the Greeks. Perhaps it was chance that dictated the choice. An *o* vowel was needed and *'ayin* was going free. Otherwise *'ayin* might have been used for *a*.

Later in the classical Greek alphabet the *o* sound was given two signs and names to match: the sign for *omicron*, the little or short *o,* and the sign for *omega*, the long or big *o*.

omicron

omega

The development of the vowel *u* is not so clear. It seems that the Semitic *wāw* for the consonant *w* became the Greek vowel sign for *u (upsilon)*. But in this case the western Greeks could pronounce the *w* sound as well as the *u* sound and they needed both. So for the *w* sound they put in a special sign called *digamma*.

Later on, it is curious to note that the *digamma* ceased to be pronounced in eastern Greek and dropped out of their alphabet, its symbol surviving as the sign for the numeral 6.

Under different conditions the Greeks might have developed at the outset more than five signs for the vowel sounds. And we might, therefore, have more than five vowel signs in our alphabet, but the development of *eta* (long *e*) and *omega* (long *o*) came too late in Greece to affect the Latin alphabet, and hence too late for our own.

In short, the Greeks fell short of complete accuracy only because they failed to insert enough signs for all the vowel sounds, long and short. And this limitation of signs for vowels is a weakness of our alphabet also.

This matter of pronunciation was a particularly difficult one for the Greeks. They were of one race but, unlike the Romans, they were far from being a united nation. They had the same language but all Greeks did not speak it exactly the same way. Every little state had its own dialect, its own peculiarities in the shape and sound of its letters.

It is not surprising, therefore, that in different parts of ancient Greece the alphabet should have developed along somewhat different lines; that almost every Greek state should have had its own alphabet. These have been broadly grouped into two main divisions: the Eastern, or Ionic, alphabet, and the Western, or Chalcidian, alphabet.

It was not until about 400 B.C. that the Eastern alphabet was officially adopted at Athens. Then little by little all of the local alphabets disappeared in favor of the Ionic, which thus became the common, classical Greek alphabet of twenty-four letters.

As might be expected in recording ancient history, there is still much controversy over the date when the Phoenician alphabet found its way into Greece. If we take the ninth century B.C., we should be reasonably safe, and even that late date allows four full centuries for the Greeks to develop their classical alphabet.

During that long time, as was the case with the

GREEK ALPHABETS
Early and Classical

SOUND VALUE	NAME	SIGN	
		Early	*Classical*
a	alpha	Α	Α
b	beta	Β	Β
g	gamma	Γ	Γ
d	delta	Δ	Δ
e	epsilon	Ε	Ε
w	(digamma)	Ϝ	
z	zeta	Ι	Ζ
h, ē	eta	Β	Η
th	theta	⊕	Θ
i	iota	⌇	Ι
k	kappa	Κ	Κ
l	lambda	Λ	Λ
m	mu	Μ	Μ
n	nu	Ν	Ν
x	xi	Ξ	Ξ
o	omikron	Ο	Ο
p	pi	Π	Π
s	(san)	Μ	
q	(koppa)	Ϙ	
r	rho	Ρ	Ρ
s	sigma	Σ	Σ
t	taw	Τ	Τ
u, ü	upsilon	Υ	Υ
ph	phi	Φ	Φ
ch	chi	Χ	Χ
ps	psi		Ψ
ō	omega		Ω

scripts of other nations, some letters had been improved, a few had been added, a few dropped from use. However, interesting though that may be, we are not concerned with a complete story of the development of the Greek alphabet nor with the similarity of some later Greek letters to our own.

We are mainly concerned with the early Greek letters because it was in the early days of the Greek alphabet that the people of Italy borrowed it—first the Etruscans, and then the Romans from them.

In addition to other things the Greeks contributed to our alphabet, they settled for us the direction of writing from left to right, but that was not done all at once. At first they wrote from right to left or alternate lines in both directions, which they called *boustrophedon*. Notice how the appearance of the letters changes with the direction of writing.

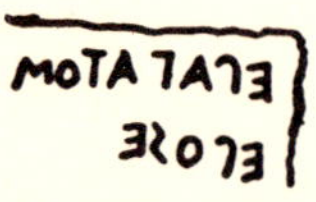

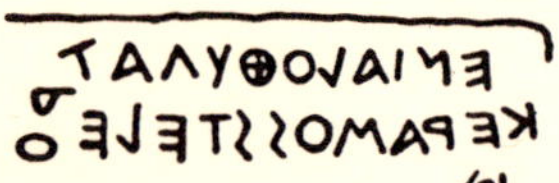

THE ROMANCE OF WRITING by K. G. Irwin

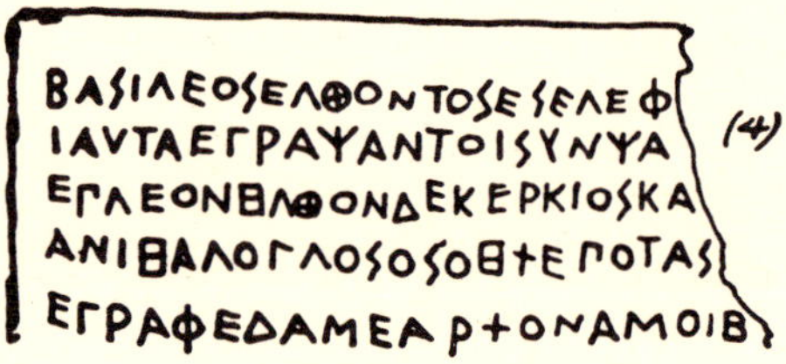

Examples of Greek writing

In example (1) and (2) the direction of writing is from right to left in Phoenician style. Now watch the direction that the E's face. In example (3) the top line runs to the right, the next line to the left, the next to the right—just as if one were plowing a field. In example (4) the direction is that of all later Greek writing, from left to right.

Important as were the contributions made by the Greeks, improvements in the art of writing did not cease with them. For one thing, their writing was all in capitals; small letters were not introduced until centuries later. In the second place, there was no space between words. Printed that way this sentence would read: PRINTEDTHATWAYTHISSENTENCEWOULDREAD. In the third place, they used no punctuation. These three elements in writing, so familiar to us, were refinements of which the early Greeks were unaware.

However, this we can say: although the Greeks did not invent the alphabet, they improved it to such a degree that their alphabet, after three thousand years, still occupies a unique and paramount place in the history of writing.

Ancient Italy
100 miles
Mantua
Spina
Felsina
Marzabotto
Fæsulæ
Pisæ
Umbri
Arretium
Cortona
Perusia
Vada
Nicæa
Elba
Marsiliana
Sabines
Volsinii
Cosa
Faleri
Volci
Veii
KYRNOS
Tarquinii
Alatia
Rome
Præneste
Ostia
Volsci
Olbia
Capua
Cumæ
Neapolis
Tarent
SARDO
Tharros
Sybaris
Croton
Carales
Locri
Panormus
Messana
Phœnicians
Motya
Rhegium
Catana
Hippo Regius
Acragas
Syracuse
Utica
Gela
Carthage
Melita
Pola
Ariminum
Salona
SPQR
ADRIATIC SEA
TYRRHENIAN SEA
Greeks
Etruscans
Etruscans
Greeks
Phœnicians
Raisz

CHAPTER TEN

The Etruscans

This is the story of ancient Rome and the Latin alphabet, the parent of our own. It is also the story of the Etruscans from whom the Romans learned their letters.

The Etruscans first appeared in Italy long before Rome was founded by the legendary Romulus and Remus. But who they were and where they came from is still one of the most baffling problems of history. Probably they migrated from Asia Minor, settled on the west coast of Italy and subdued the natives of that area.

At any rate, their loose-leagued confederacy of city states appears to have included the whole of northern Italy down to the Tiber, where an Etruscan dynasty reigned in Rome for a century or more. Rivalry between the Etruscans and the Romans for control of Italy continued for nearly five hundred years until the power of Etruria was finally destroyed and their country absorbed into the growing Roman domain.

The earliest written records about the Etruscans come from Greek and Roman chroniclers who tended to write of them with envy and scorn tinged with a reluctant admiration, for the Etruscans were naval fighters and formidable warriors. They were creators and conquerors of cities, adventurers, skilled artisans and successful traders.

Unfortunately, the written Etruscan record is all but useless as a guide to their life and culture because their language still remains a mystery and is still unintelligible. Scholars can read Etruscan, but they cannot connect the words to meanings. Inscriptions can be read but not understood.

Why should that be? With many Etruscan inscriptions for the scholars to work on, why can they not interpret the language? In short, why should the language of the Etruscans remain the "enigma of all Italian enigmas"?

One reason is that all the longer texts are monolingual. Champollion had the Greek text for his key in deciphering the Rosetta Stone. Another reason is that the Latin-Etruscan bilingual texts exist only in the very short burial inscriptions, which are of little help. Proper names, names of parents and kin, official titles, dates and the oft repeated words *died,* or *deceased,* are all that can be extracted from them.

But another kind of record happily survived and for that, as is the case with other peoples, we must turn to the archeologists. From them we learn that the Etruscans were a settled and civilized people from the eighth century B.C. at least. We learn, also, that the Etruscan buildings were on a magnificent scale.

In one tomb the gold work alone would stock a large jeweler's shop. In many tombs the walls are covered with vividly painted frescoes of their daily life. Chariot races, dancing, wrestling, and many other sports and pleasures are all depicted.

Gaiety marks the scene from a rich man's tomb. The Etruscans seem to have been enthusiastic sportsmen, gamblers and musicians. The ruling class loved life and lived it joyously.

It was from the Etruscans that the Romans took their architecture and other fundamentals of civilization. It was from them that the Romans got the idea of paved roads, sewers and aqueducts, of the circus, the chariot race and the purple border of the toga. Their laws formed the basis of Roman laws; their military system was a model for the invincible Roman legion that turned Rome into the master of the world.

Most important of all, it was from the Etruscans that the Romans got their alphabet—not from the Greek colonists in southern Italy, a theory which was formerly taken for granted. But formerly, too little was made of the Etruscan influence on the Romans.

True, the primitive Romans were practically surrounded by the Greek alphabet. It was used by the Greeks to the south of them, by the Etruscans to the north. More exactly, however, the Etruscans were not only north of them but upon them, for in the early days Etruria ruled Rome.

Some say the Etruscans brought their alphabet with them when first they came to Italy, and there are other theories about its origin. So now we come.to a little object found not so long ago. It does not solve the mystery of how or when the Etruscan alphabet came into being, but from it we can safely assume two things—that the Etruscans used the alphabet at a very early date, and that it is of Greek origin.

That object, called the Marsiliana Abecedarium, found in a tomb at Marsiliana, is an ivory writing tablet, about 3½ inches by 2 inches, with a raised border. The sunken part of the tablet once contained a thin coating of wax on which the written letters were traced with a sharp pointed stylus. Carefully incised in the ivory of the raised upper border is a complete alphabet of twenty-six letters. Probably it was the copybook of some Etruscan youngster.

This important tablet is dated about 700 B.C., a mere hundred years or so after the Greeks bor-

Marsiliana abecedarium   *Courtesy of Antichita dell' Etruria, Florence, Italy*

ALPHABETS
Early Greek to Etruscan

SOUND VALUE	SIGN	
	Greek	*Etruscan*
a	𐤀	𐤀
b	𐤁	𐤁
g	𐤂	𐤂
d	𐤃	𐤃
e	𐤄	𐤄
w	𐤅	𐤅
z	𐤆	𐤆
h	𐤇	𐤇
th	𐤈	𐤈
i	𐤉	𐤉
k	𐤊	𐤊
l	𐤋	𐤋
m	𐤌	𐤌
n	𐤍	𐤍
x	𐤎	𐤎
o	𐤏	𐤏
p	𐤐	𐤐
s	𐤑	𐤑
q	𐤒	𐤒
r	𐤓	𐤓
s	𐤔	𐤔
t	𐤕	𐤕
y	Υ	Υ
x		Χ
ph	Φ	Φ
ch	Χ	Ψ

rowed the Phoenician letters. The fact that an Etruscan of that early time should be using a fine writing tablet made of imported ivory would seem to indicate that writing was already well-established in Etruria at a time when the Greek colonies did not exist or before they could have exercised much, if any, cultural influence on Etruria or Rome.

The evidence, therefore, seems to show that the Etruscan alphabet was the earliest alphabet used in Italy. Furthermore, that the Etruscans borrowed their alphabet from the Greeks is evident from a comparison of the letters.

Note how closely the shapes of the Etruscan letters correspond to the early Greek. Etruscan writing goes like the Semitic and early Greek alphabets, nearly always from right to left. That is why the letter *a* on the Marsiliana tablet appears to be the last letter in the alphabet.

There is, of course, much more to tell about the Etruscans and their writing. The archaic form of their alphabet, as happened in Greece, was modified over the centuries until about 400 B.C. the classical Etruscan alphabet took its final form, having twenty letters—four vowels and sixteen consonants.

They used the Greek *gamma* for *g* and added a new letter with the sign 8, meaning *f*, a sound which abounded in Etruscan.

However, it was the Etruscan alphabet in its early form which became the link between Greece and Rome. So it must be admitted that the Etruscans contributed little to the alphabet except for passing on the Greek letters to Rome.

CHAPTER ELEVEN

The Latin Alphabet

Just how and when the urge to write first spread among the Romans we do not know. The earliest surviving specimen of writing in Latin has been dated about 600 B.C. Probably when Etruria was still dominant in Italy, during the seventh century B.C., the alphabet was introduced to the Romans.

This earliest surviving specimen of Latin writing is incised on a gold fibula, or brooch, discovered at Praeneste (modern Palestrina) not far from Rome. Written in the archaic manner, it reads from right to left; if reversed to read from left to right, it would read *MANIOS MED FHE-FHAKED NUMASIOI,* which means, "Manius made me for Numasius".

Praeneste fibula

After D. Diringer

Thus we see that the Etruscans brought an early Greek alphabet to Italy a very short time after the Greeks adopted the Semitic Phoenician alphabet in the ninth century B.C. and that the Romans borrowed the alphabet from the Etruscans a mere century or so later; or it might be more accurate to say that they were taught it when they were under Etruscan influence. That was some three hundred years before the Greeks and Etruscans had perfected their own alphabets, and it means that the Romans did not take over the alphabet at the point where the Greeks and Etruscans had finished.

Since the alphabet was still crude when the Romans began to use it, it would appear that the Greeks, Etruscans and the Latins were working out their alphabets at the same time. The Latins, however, must have been influenced by the Greeks as well as the Etruscans, because Greek colonies were not far from Rome in its early days.

Roughly speaking, therefore, the Latin alpha-

EARLY ALPHABETS
(Letter signs given in Latin order)

SEMITIC	GREEK	ETRUSCAN	LATIN
			A
			B
			C
			D
			E
			F
			H
			I
			K
			L
			M
			N
			O
			P
			Q
			R
			S
			T
			V
			X

Letters first adopted by Romans   20
Additions — B.C.

SEMITIC	GREEK	ETRUSCAN	LATIN
			G
			Y
			Z

Standard Roman Alphabet   23
Medieval Additions

SEMITIC	GREEK	ETRUSCAN	LATIN
			J
			U
			W (VV)

bet was the Semitic-Greek-Etruscan alphabet. But that does not mean that the Romans were mere imitators. They used what was suitable for their language and manner of speaking it. The Romans went a long way toward developing an alphabet which became the basis for our own. They continued to develop their alphabet long after the Greeks and Etruscans had perfected their alphabets.

The direction of writing on the Praeneste fibula is from right to left. Even the very ancient custom of *boustrophedon* writing still persisted when the Romans began to write. But later they established their order of writing from left to right, probably due to Greek influence.

Therefore, on the preceding chart the Latin letters are shown in the way to which we are accustomed—namely, to face for writing from left to right. They are also given in capitals because the ancient Romans used only the letter forms which we call capitals. It was not for many centuries that writing shifted from the formal, dignified capitals to the simpler, smaller, and more rounded letter forms made so readily with pen strokes on parchment and vellum.

As shown on the chart, the Romans adopted twenty letters from the early Etruscan alphabet, some with hardly any change in shape, others somewhat modified in shape. Another three of the twenty-six early Etruscan letters, as we shall see later, were converted by the Romans into numerals. *Theta,* for example, developed into another symbol, then became C, the initial letter of Centum for 100.

The Romans kept the ancient letter F (called by the Greeks *digamma* or double *gamma*) which the Greek alphabet had dropped after a time. It represented a *v* sound not needed for Greek pronunciation, but the Romans finally conferred upon it the sound value it has today.

The Romans retained Q but, as stated below, used it only before consonantal U; that is, only when U was followed by a vowel. It is still employed in that way in European languages, at least. There is no reason why Q should not have a definite sound by itself so that we might write "qeen," "qick" and "qote" instead of queen, quick and quote. But the ancient Etruscans and Romans established the usage of QU and we have never broken with that tradition.

Now for the K, C, and G story.

The Roman alphabet had one peculiar feature which they adopted from the Etruscans, who used K only before A, Q only before U and also used C (the Greek *gamma* or *g*) for the sound *k*. Thus the Romans had three letters for the *k* sound. And we write "cat," "king" and "qu" using three letters for the one sound *k*, a super-abundance of *k* sounds which the Etruscans foisted upon the world more than twenty-five hundred years ago.

But the ancient Romans had no letter to differentiate *g* from *k*. They used the letter *c* to express the sound of *g* as well as of *c*. In course of time they realized and corrected this defect by inventing the modified sign G for *g*.

Strange to say, they did not assign the *k* sound to the letter K. The *k* sound had, in fact, taken such complete possession of the letter C that the original and legitimate owner, G, was looked upon as the intruder and made to find another home. It went into the alphabet, not in the third position where the Greek *gamma* had been, but in the seventh place, where the Greek *zeta* had been located. The Romans had dropped the *zeta*.

This new letter G first came into existence in the fourth or third century B.C. For the shape of this new letter the Romans put a little "beard" on the letter C to make G.

It is interesting to note that even after the new letter G had been added, the Romans continued to use C to represent G in such familiar abbreviations as CN (for Gnaeus) and C (for Gaius). It is also interesting that K eventually disappeared from the language, except as an abbreviation in a few words beginning with KA (e.g., *Kalendae*). But when the Roman alphabet was adopted into English and German, K again came into honor. And so we see that letters, like human beings, have their ups and downs.

The Y and Z stories are also interesting.

In later times, when Greek culture was penetrating the Roman world and Greek words were being introduced into the Latin language, the need for a new letter was felt. So the symbol Y (the Greek *upsilon*) was adopted for the sound *y* from the contemporary Greek alphabet.

Under the same Greek influences, the Romans added still another letter by restoring Z. Centuries earlier, as we know, the Greek *zeta* had been discarded by the Romans as useless. When Z was put back into the alphabet, it had to go to the very end of the list because its old place had been given to G and then C. Such is the struggle for existence.

Thus the Roman alphabet was finally completed with twenty-three letters. We miss our J, U, and W. These three letters were added in the Middle Ages.

The Romans used I (the Greek vowel *iota*) both as a vowel and a consonant. The addition of a curved tail to I added the new letter J which took over the consonantal sound of *i*. Likewise the Romans used V (the Greek vowel *upsilon*) as both a vowel and a consonant. The rounding out of V to U added another new letter to represent the vowel sound *u*.

As to W, its form and its English name, "double U," show that it was made up from VV to take over the old function of V.

What a long and full history the Semitic letter *waw* has had! The Greeks used it for both their vowel *upsilon* and their consonant *digamma*. From Roman and medieval times it has come down to us as the basis for our F, U, V, W, and Y.

To discuss in full the way that the sound values for J, U, and W developed would require pages of explanation, and that also applies to many letters of the Latin alphabet. However, such a lengthy and technical exposition hardly belongs in a brief outline of the evolution of our alphabet. An understanding of consonants, vowels, and semi-vowels, of the sounds for which letters are used in any particular language, is of more interest to the philologist, to the student of languages, than to the general reader who knows from his own experience how differently the same language is spoken in various parts of the United States, not to mention England. That subject alone would fill a sizable book.

A still larger volume would be required to describe how the Latin alphabet was used by many nations for their languages. The Egyptian system of writing, the Semitic and Greek alphabets, were each designed for a single language. The Latin alphabet, on the other hand, which was first developed for a single language, was adapted to the largest number of different tongues over a wide geographical area. With minor variations it is now employed for writing in Czech, Dutch, English, Finnish, French, German, Hungarian, Polish, Turkish, Welsh and many other languages and dialects.

To tell how this came about would involve a study of the political and social unrest throughout Europe when new nationalities began to assert themselves and the national vernaculars broke down the prevailing Latin language into the various languages which survive today. It would involve a study of each language and how the Latin letters were made to fit its vocabulary, its manner of speech, its pronunciation and inflections; a study of the wandering of words from nation to nation, their changes in meaning and pronunciation, and other technicalities which do not belong here.

The history of the Latin alphabet after the first century B.C. consists not only in the adaptation of that alphabet to various languages but also in the external transformation of the single letters and the development of national scripts.

We read about the *majuscules,* or capital letters, which the ancient Romans used for so long a time; about the *uncials* (from the Latin word *uncia,* inch) which were letters of exaggerated size and more rounded in form; about the *semi-uncials* and the *miniscules,* or small letters.

We read about the cursive or running style of writing to which we are accustomed; about scripts which were a mixture of *majuscules, uncials,* and cursive letters, for no one style was used exclusively at any one period.

Long before the *uncial* style finally went out of use, its successor was developing, just as the *uncials* themselves developed before the *majuscule* capitals entirely lost their vogue. First came the semi- or half-*uncials,* an intermediate step on the way to the *miniscules,* or small letters. It was the half-*uncial* style which was carried into Ireland by Saint Patrick.

There is nothing unusual in this gradual change in the forms of the Latin letters, for, as we have already seen, the forms of letters throughout the ages have been determined very largely by the materials and tools used for writing. The letters, as they journeyed over the centuries from land to land, were at the same time making another journey. From stone and chisel they went to papyrus and reed pen, from papyrus to wax tablet and stylus, from wax tablet to parchment and vellum, and finally to paper on which flowing rounded strokes could be made with quill and pen.

Another factor which led to change in the letter

forms was the perfectly natural impulse of scribes to write more smoothly and rapidly, and this impulse was encouraged by the increasing use of the smooth-surfaced parchments and vellums. Then too, as might be expected, there were innovators among the scribes who were no longer trained in the ancient traditions of their craft.

Scribes, drawn from the ranks of public writers, notaries, scriveners, conveyancers and others, wanted a utilitarian script which could be used for everyday purposes—legal, commercial and social. Some straight lines gave way to curves, and distinguishing strokes in some of the letters were extended above or below the line of writing. For example, the straight lines of M and N were easily modified into curves resembling those of our *m* and *n,* and the vertical stroke of P grew downward to make p.

In those troubled times following the slow dis-

Scriptorium with scribe at work

integration of the Roman Empire, while the church was growing in power, the writing and transcribing of books took refuge in monasteries, cloisters and other religious establishments. The scribes were no longer hired men paid by an author or publisher but clerics and monks who worked for the church.

Each center of book production developed its own style of penmanship. Thus there developed the five national hands known as Italic, or Lombardic, Merovingian in France, Visigothic in Spain, Germanic, and Insular in the British Isles. Each of them gave rise to several varieties.

Even when writing was done on the same material, as parchment or vellum, the letters did not keep to the same form, but were constantly changing. Since the advent of printing, however, the book form of our letters has become definitely set and fixed. There is little likelihood of any marked change in the future such as the changes made during the centuries of evolution under the hands of the scribes.

CHAPTER TWELVE

Numerals

Just as the first attempts at writing came long after people had learned to talk, so the first efforts at the representation of numbers by symbols came long after people had learned to count on their fingers. Although numerals are in no sense a part of the alphabet which has come down to us from ancient times, they have become an indispensable part of the system of symbols with which we write. Hence, it would appear that the story of numerals has a definite place in the history of writing.

In many books it has been customary to number the chapters by the Roman numerals: I, II, III, IV, etc. The pages, on the other hand, are usually numbered by the so-called Arabic system of notation: 1, 2, 3, 4, etc.

But the ancient world had methods of writing numbers other than the more or less familiar Roman and Hindu-Arabic numerals. Indeed, a long book could be written on the methods used in Egypt, Mesopotamia and other places. Therefore, in this book the story of numerals is limited to the Roman and to our own, which developed from the Hindu-Arabic numerals.

The principle behind what we know as the Roman system is perhaps the most widespread method, historically speaking. The smallest numbers are simple repetitions of 1.

Fundamentally different from all these methods is the place value notation of our own system, where neither 12 nor 21 represents 1 plus 2 or 2 plus 1, but 1 times 10 plus 2, and 2 times 10 plus 1, respectively. Hence the position of a number symbol determines its value and consequently a limited number of symbols suffices to express numbers, however large, without the need for repetitions or creation of new, higher symbols. The invention of this place value notation is undoubtedly one of the most fertile inventions of humanity. It can be properly compared with the invention of the small number of letters for an alphabet as contrasted to the use of thousands of symbols for picture-writing or the hundreds needed for syllabic writing.

Both the Roman and Arabic symbols have one thing in common. Unlike the letters of an alphabet, they have no phonetic value whatsoever. They do not "spell" the names of the numbers. They are literally pictures of them. For instance, the symbol "5" means the same in any language, whether it is pronounced five, fünf, cinq, and so on.

The symbols used for the Roman numerals are nothing less than pictures of the fingers held up in counting and they are called digits from the Latin "digitus," the finger. The Roman "V" is simply a picture of the open palm—one side representing the thumb; the other side, the four fingers. The symbol "X" for ten was merely two "V's" connected at the points.

Every schoolboy knows that IV is one less than V and that VI, VII are, respectively, one and two digits more than V. Incidentally, the subtraction method of using IV (instead of IIII) for 4 and IX (instead of VIIII) for 9 seems to have developed later than the addition method of VI and XII for 6 and 12.

The Romans, as we have seen, rejected the letters *theta, phi* and *chi* in the Etruscan alphabet because there were no sounds in Latin to correspond to them. Having no use for them as letters, the Romans retained them to represent numbers. How these three symbols may have developed into shapes for the larger numerals is shown below.

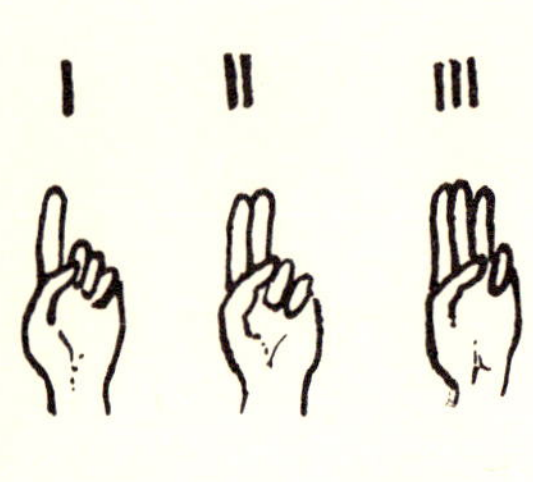

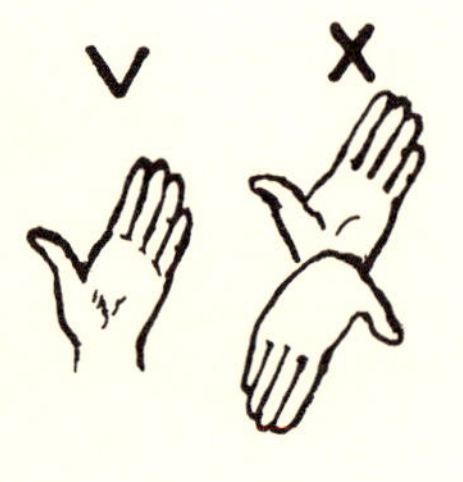

Etruscan	Roman
chi ↓	↓ - ⊥ - L thus L for 50
Theta ⊗	⊙ - Ϲ - C thus C (centum) for 100
Phi φ	(ı) - ⅭⅮ - ⋒ thus M (mille) for 1000

D for 500 was taken from one half of Phi

It is obvious that the use of Roman numerals in calculations must have been quite awkward. Actually, calculations were not made in Roman numbers from written-down figures as they are today, but just how the Romans added, divided, subtracted and multiplied does not belong in the history of writing.

Roman numerals, nevertheless, have not been wholly discarded. We still use them today. Convention still sanctions their use for dates, for chapters, on title pages, in monumental inscriptions, and in other limited ways.

For everyday use we employ the so-called Arabic numerals, so it is with them that our interest mainly lies. Their history is buried in the remote past of the mystical and romantic East. The question of their origin is not a simple one. According to the most generally accepted view, Arabic numerals originated in India.

It seems clear that the Hindu numerals became known to Arabic scholars and that they reached the schools of Northern Africa and the great Moorish universities of Spain, which was the only Moslem country in Western Europe at that time. The Moors in Spain are said to have introduced these numerals into Europe somewhere around the twelfth century A.D.

But they did not come into anything approaching general use for a long time. The simplest calculations continued to require the aid of an abacus, and arithmetical notation was limited by the cumbersome Roman numerals.

As in the case of our letters, the Hindu-Arabic numerals passed through a succession of changes before they became standardized into the shapes we use today. How the shapes developed has been variously explained, but no complete explanation has found general acceptance. However, a more or less plausible explanation for the shapes of our 2 and 3 is that they developed from horizontal strokes indicating the numbers. Thus the strokes = and ≡, when written rapidly without lifting the pen, became our 2 and 3.

Europe took a long time to settle finally upon what shapes the numerals should be. Europeans also took a long, long time to learn how to use them—in particular, those of the zero and of the place value notation.

We take the zero for granted, but at first there was no zero at all. Indeed, what is a zero? Nothing. An empty place. It took people many centuries to think up a way to represent an empty place. It could be done on an abacus board by leaving a space empty; this method served long and well in making calculations.

The early Romans had no zero, although it existed elsewhere much earlier. But there are too many conflicting opinions and claims to fix an exact date and place for this great invention.

Ptolemy was a celebrated Greek astronomer and mathematician of the second century A.D. In his *Almagest* we find a special sign for zero, used exactly as our zero. Indeed, the Arabic form for the zero (a circle with a bar over it and related forms) was simply taken from Greek astronomical manuscripts.

Only in the Byzantine manuscripts do we find the bare 0-like shape which suggests an arbitrarily invented symbol to indicate an empty space. Other ancient examples of the zero symbol varied some-what.

Even before the zero came into general use, that other great invention for giving place value to the numerals had been made. The sexagesimal place value notation is a striking feature of the Babylonian system. This method became the es-sential tool in the development of their mathe-matical astronomy, whence it spread to the Greeks and then to the Hindus, who contributed the final step—namely, the use of the place value notation for the decimal units. It is this system which we use today.

The place value notation, as we have seen, makes it possible for any given numeral to repre-sent not only itself, but in a combination with other numerals, ten times itself, a hundred times itself, etc. When we write 5,300,375 the first figure 5 is written exactly the same way as the last, but while the last 5 represents only itself, the first represents millions. Put in another way, the 6 in 6,666 has four values: the absolute value of 6; 10 times 6, or 60; 100 times 6, or 600; and 1,000 times 6, or 6,000.

The place value of numbers is simple to us. As in the case of the zero, however, it took the Europeans a long, long time to learn its use, and they experimented with other systems besides the decimal system, based on the primitive method of counting by fingers—for example, the sexagesimal system, founded on the number 60. From it we get the division of the circumference into 360 parts, which originated in Babylonian astronomy. And the duodecimal system which obstinately survives in English measurements today: twelve pence in a shilling, twelve units in a dozen, twelve dozen in a gross, twelve inches in a foot. Thirteen, on the other hand, refused to be divided by any number and became disreputable and unlucky forever.

According to some, the plus sign $(+)$ and minus sign $(-)$ first appeared in the fifteenth century and the present way of writing common fractions seems to have been an Arab invention.

At any rate, this much we can say without dispute. The symbols for the numerals and their use with the zero and place value came long after the alphabet was in general use throughout Europe and in England.

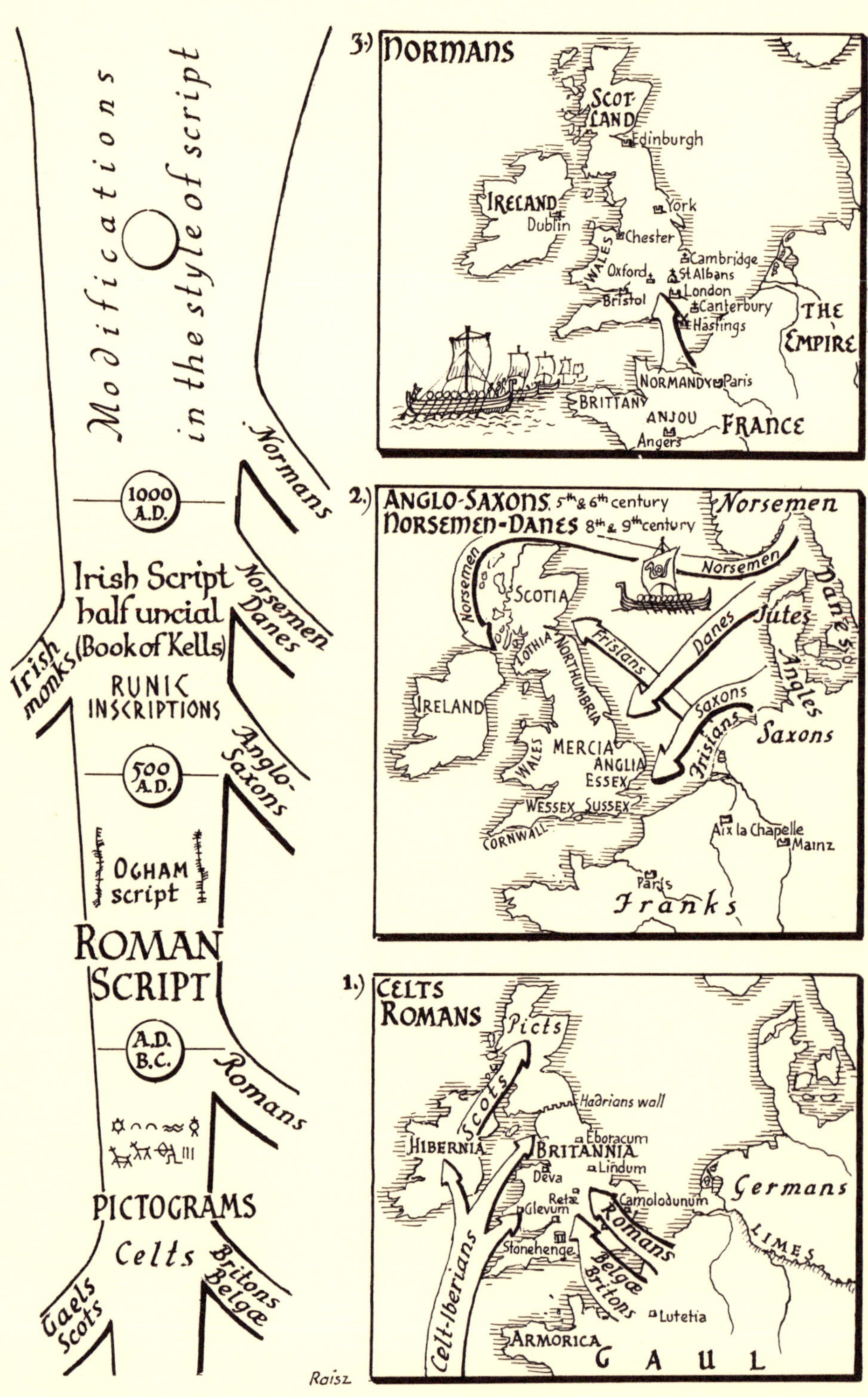

Modifications in the style of script

1000 A.D.
Normans

Irish Script
half uncial
(Book of Kells)
Irish monks
Norsemen Danes

RUNIC INSCRIPTIONS

500 A.D.
Anglo-Saxons

OGHAM script

ROMAN SCRIPT

A.D. B.C.
Romans

PICTOGRAMS

Celts
Gaels Scots
Britons Belgæ

3.) NORMANS
SCOTLAND
Edinburgh
IRELAND
Dublin
York
WALES
Chester
Oxford
Cambridge
St Albans
London
Bristol
Canterbury
Hastings
THE EMPIRE
NORMANDY
Paris
BRITTANY
ANJOU
Angers
FRANCE

2.) ANGLO-SAXONS 5th & 6th century
NORSEMEN-DANES 8th & 9th century
Norsemen
Norsemen
Norsemen
SCOTIA
Danes
Jutes
Angles
Frisians
Saxons
Saxons
IRELAND
LOTHIA NORTHUMBRIA
WALES
MERCIA
ANGLIA
ESSEX
Frisians
WESSEX SUSSEX
CORNWALL
Aix la Chapelle
Mainz
Paris
Franks

1.) CELTS ROMANS
Picts
Scots
Hadrians wall
HIBERNIA
Eboracum
BRITANNIA
Deva
Lindum
Reta
Camolodunum
Glevum
Romans
GERMANS
Stonehenge
Belgæ
Britons
LIMES
Celt-Iberians
Lutetia
ARMORICA
GAUL
Raisz

CHAPTER THIRTEEN

The English Alphabet

At the start of this chapter, it should be noted that many people call our alphabet the English alphabet even though it is largely the Latin alphabet with a few additions. Where the term English alphabet is used, it should be understood as meaning the Latin alphabet as adapted to the English language.

The history of each country has had an influence on the way its system of writing developed. In few cases, however, have the history of a country, the events which shaped its course, the people who occupied its land and the languages they spoke had a more pronounced influence on the way its writing developed than was the case with England. English history and English writing are inseparable.

The written history of Britain really begins with Julius Caesar about half a century before the birth of Christ, but its conquest came under the Emperor Claudius about one century later. For some four centuries England was under Roman rule. Thereafter it absorbed Saxon, Dane and Norman in order, and transformed them into its own English race, creating its own spoken and written English language.

The greater portion of the population of Britain at the time of the Roman conquest belonged to the widespread Celtic-speaking nations which overran so much of Europe in the last six centuries before Christ. The pre-Celtic people of Britain are spoken of collectively as Iberian, although they consisted of many different races. In the end the Celtic-speaking people and Iberians more or less intermingled, but, as happened on all such occasions in Britain, many of the conquered found refuge in the mountains to the north and west.

At least two big waves of Celtic invasion can be distinguished.

First came the Gaels, among whom were the Irish or the Scots—Scottus simply meant Irishman. Later on, bands of these wild Irish tribesmen, the Scots, migrated across the sea and established themselves in the northern part of the British island. The ancient people dwelling there, the Picts, about whom little is known, gradually gave up their language, and the land was called Scotia, Scotland.

Second came the Brythons, or Britons proper, among whom were the Belgae and other tribes whom the Romans found spread over southern England. Because they also spoke a Celtic language, the term Celt is generally used to designate the native population which inhabited Britain when the Romans conquered the island.

For almost four centuries the Romans occupied Britain, or rather that part of the island which we now call England and Wales. Again there was a mingling of races and, as was usual in Roman provinces, the work of pacification and the adoption by the people of Roman civilization followed close upon the conquest. For more than three hundred years England was a comparatively peaceful Roman province although its borders were troubled from time to time by uprisings and barbarian invasions.

The Roman Empire had grown out of a city-state, its civilization was based upon city life, so in Britain old cities grew in importance and new cities rose over the land. It is probable, therefore, that in the cities and towns Latin became the standard language and that the Latin way of writing was used by the native town dwellers.

However, in the rural districts and more remote parts of the country, as well as in the highlands of Ireland and Scotland, a large portion of the original population still survived, with the Celtic language in common use and their folkways almost undisturbed through the whole Roman period.

So here it would seem appropriate to touch upon a system of writing used by the Celts of

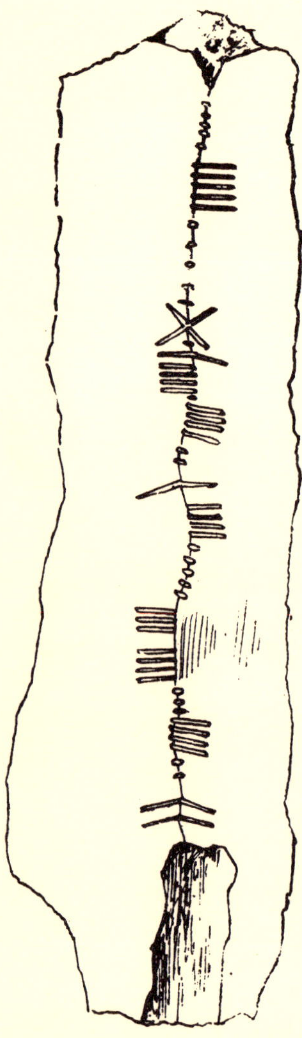

From the Ogham inscribed monuments of the GAEDHIL *by R. R. Brosh*

Britain and Ireland, even though it had no part whatsoever in the development of our English script.

It was a peculiar kind of script called *Ogham* or *Ogam*. Ogham writing was done along the edge of a stone or piece of wood, as shown on this Ogham stone:

The letters were formed by horizontal or diagonal parallel strokes which varied in number from one to five, and were drawn to the left or right or through a vertical line. The Ogham alphabet, if the inscription were turned on its side and a horizontal line used instead of the vertical line, would have the following appearance:

After Holgar Pederson

Note that the alphabet is arranged in a remarkably regular way and is divided into groups with five letters in each group. The vowels appear in a group of their own.

Oghams were used only for Celtic writing. They are found all over Ireland and in Wales and in Cornwall as well, but here the language betrays the fact that they are from the hands of Irishmen. We also have Ogham inscriptions from Scotland which no doubt came from the Irish who migrated to Scotland and gave Scotland its name.

Ogham writing, then, is a special Irish system, although there has been no lack of fantastic conjecture regarding its origin. It seems likely that

Ogham writing was an attempt to make a new kind of script, based on the knowledge of a pre-existing alphabet, probably Latin. But Irish tradition, as was the tradition in other countries, attributes its discovery to a divine being, to Ogma, a late Irish mythological figure whose name is identical with that of the Gaulish god of eloquence.

Not only is its origin obscure but also it is very difficult to date its beginning. In their datings, scholars vary from the second century to the fifth century A.D.

In any case, Ogham inscriptions extend over a period of several centuries. The Ogham period begins in the heathen period and Ogham monuments continued to be set up in Christian times, so that we find stones with double inscriptions, partly in Ogham and partly in the Latin alphabet, which came in with Christianity.

When legible, Ogham inscriptions are valuable in giving us our earliest Irish and Welsh texts and their value to linguists is far from negligible.

During the fourth century A.D. the Roman Empire everywhere experienced increasing difficulties in protecting its frontiers against barbaric races. The Teutonic conquest of Gaul cut Britain off from Rome, leaving the Romano-British peoples to defend themselves against savage attacks by the Angles, Saxons and Jutes from across the water. Britain fell a prey to the invaders. By the year 440 the Romans had withdrawn from their island colony.

After Britain was cast adrift from the Roman

Empire, a curtain of historical darkness seems to have descended upon the island. When it was lifted several centuries later, the Germanic tribes from the opposite shore had converted southern Britain into England, while the Celtic-speaking people held to the hills in Wales, Cornwall and Scotland. The Celts in Britain and Ireland did not lose their language. They borrowed a number of Latin loan-words, but the vigor of the Celtic language did not diminish.

The attempt of the Romans to Latinize the Celtic civilization had broken down; perhaps there were too few Romans. In short, the Roman occupation intervened between the coming of the Celts and the coming of the Teutonic Anglo-Saxons and delayed the Teutonic conquest by perhaps two hundred years. But the Romans, after centuries, had contributed little to the stock of institutions which constitute the heritage of Englishmen.

The year 449 A.D., the traditional date of the arrival of the first Teutonic settlers, represents the entrance of its real founders into Britain. It is especially unfortunate that contemporary records are almost lacking for the period during which the very foundations of English culture were being laid by the Anglo-Saxons, who brought their Germanic civilization with them.

It is impossible to tell how far the population became a mixed race of Teutons and the old inhabitants of Britain, but there can be no doubt that a large portion of the island's population sprang from the newcomers. Their language, religion, government, and, in the main, their customs rapidly superseded those of Celtic and Roman Britain.

Of less lasting importance, the Anglo-Saxons brought to Britain the earliest form of Germanic writing, known as *runes.* The name means mystery-secret and shows the sense of mystery which was attached to the beginnings of writing everywhere. Runes probably had their source in one or the other of the alphabets of Rome or Greece, perhaps in both. Some say they were derived from a late Northern Etruscan alphabet.

The oldest runic alphabet was used throughout the whole Germanic territory. It contained twenty-four symbols in three series of eight, arranged probably according to a magical principal later forgotten. The alphabet ran as follows:

ᚠᚢᚦᚨᚱ᛭ᚷᚹ : ᚺᚾᛁᛃᛇᛈᛉᛋ : ᛏᛒᛖᛗᛚᛜᛟᛞ

f u þ a r k g w h n i j ɛ p z s t b e u l ng o d

After the sounds of the first six letters, this alphabet is sometimes called *futhark,* a name which appears inconsistent because of the third letter. This letter is shown in two ways. According to Professor Bloomfield, "People who saw the runic letter in ancient English writings but did not know its value as *th,* took it to be a form of the letter Y and arrived at the notion that the article 'the' was in older English 'ye'." This may explain our use of ye for the, as in "Ye old tavern" for "The old tavern."

The oldest runic inscriptions date from about 300 A.D. Later as the Church of Rome extended its influence and the Germanic peoples were Christianized, they gave up the runes in favor of the Latin alphabet.

In England, however, runic writing continued in use for a much longer time than elsewhere except in Scandinavia. The heathen Anglo-Saxons used it for relatively short inscriptions, chiefly of a magic or religious character, such as epitaphs. The following is the top line of an Anglo-Saxon runic inscription, with the Roman transcription, from a whalebone box known as "Frank's Casket," now in the British Museum:

ROMWALUSANDREUMWALUSTWŒGEN

After A. C. Moorhouse

But runic writing was not used to take down annals or to transcribe the epics sung by minstrel and bard. Hence for several centuries there extends a great darkness over an important page in English history.

The conquered had to learn the language of their masters; there was no need for their masters to learn the language of the conquered. Thus it came about that Latin and Celtic yielded to the speech of the invaders, except in the few places where Celtic-Gaelic speech, as we all know, has survived and is still used today.

Not until some two hundred years after the Saxon invasion do we hear the marching chant of Augustine and his monks when they came to convert the island to Christianity. With them they brought back the Latin alphabet and written record, so may we not reword the oft repeated phrase about the Roman legions by saying, "Wherever the Roman Church went, their writing followed."

Only in Celtic Wales and Ireland did Christianity survive the Saxon invasion, but the Welsh Christians seem to have hated the Saxon intruders too much to try to save their souls. Nevertheless, both Welsh and Irish must have assisted in the conversion of England, for St. Patrick was a Romanized Briton.

At the time of the conquest, the Anglo-Saxon language, except for brief runic inscriptions, was not a written language. It was Augustine and his monks who brought with them their distinctive Irish script and caused the language to become a written one. Then, with the foundation of cathedral and monastic schools, English literature awoke to a new life. We read of The Venerable Bede, the most famous of the early Saxon writers, and his *Ecclesiastical History*. We read of the poet Caedmon, who wrote in English verse.

We read about King Alfred the Great, who saved England for the Saxons against the onslaught of the Vikings. Alfred was one of the greatest of all English monarchs, but probably his most conspicuous work was the reestablishment of education and literature after their decay during the ravages of the Danes. The old literary and learned life of the monasteries, represented by Bede and Caedmon, had disappeared. King Alfred made a new center of learning at his capital of Winchester.

Alfred's zealous activities in the cause of education and his own writings served to establish

Anglo-Saxon, or Old English, as a settled literary language.

However, every language undergoes a slow but unceasing process of change. The fourteenth century English of Chaucer is unintelligible to most of us. The ninth century English of King Alfred, of which we have contemporary manuscript records, may seem to us like a foreign language.

And yet the similarity of Old English to modern English can be recognized. As an example, a few words from the Anglo-Saxon Chronicle of the year 1005 may be taken:

Her on thyssum geare waes se mycla hungor
Here in this   year was so great famine

Alfred wrote a history of England, not in Latin, as he might have done, but in the language of England. True, he used Latin letters, but he also used two of the old runes which were needed to adapt the Latin alphabet to the Anglo-Saxon tongue. There was nothing unusual about that, for we have seen how alphabets develop from other alphabets by adding new letters or changing some of the old.

The story of how these two runes got into the English alphabet goes back before Alfred was born. They were two important letter-sounds not found in the Latin but needed in the English speech. These letters had the Saxon names of *wen* and *thorn,* each letter representing the sound that formed the first part of its name.

The old English priests, in the eighth century, when they took to writing in English, retained these two runic characters, the so-called *thorn* sign and the *wen,* since the Latin did not provide letters for these sounds. It was only after the Norman conquest that English writers gave up these letters in favor of the combinations *th* and *vv,* whence our *w.*

At this point it may not be amiss to give a short resumé of the differing effects made by the successive invading peoples upon the languages of Britain. As we have seen, the Celtic language survived in Britain under four centuries of Roman domination.

On the other hand, when English was brought to the British Isles by the Jutes, Angles and Saxons in the fifth century, presumably there was a preponderance of Celtic speakers and a minority of Germanic invaders, as was the case with the Romans. Yet the effect on the language was quite the opposite, for the English language of the minority survived and ousted the Celtic language of the majority. Apart from place names (London, Thames), only those Celtic words remained for which the English had no readily available term.

Unlike Celtic several centuries earlier, the onslaught of the Vikings (Norsemen and Danes) left a considerable imprint on the English language. This imprint was not on the higher elements of culture, as was the later Norman French influence, but extended through much of the everyday vocabulary with such borrowed words as *gift, husband, root, skill, skin,* etc.

The French Normans wrote a different story upon the language. French became the speech of culture, of the government and law, of the court and camp. From the French were borrowed such government terms as *council, crown, minister* and *parliament*; legal terms, as *court, jury, plaintiff*; military words, as *armor, banner, siege*. For titles, *duke, marquis, viscount* were borrowed; only the native *earl* was kept, but the earl's wife is a *countess*.

Yet English remained the spoken tongue of the masses, and eventually the inertia of the masses prevailed over the activities of statesmen and scholars. A few upper-class Normans maintained positions of prestige for a time but gradually were replaced by speakers of English, or they themselves learned English.

English survived even though its vocabulary was profoundly modified by the loss of some English words and by the addition of French words. But the process of change, as we have seen, is something inherent in the life of any language. And alphabetic signs, as might be expected, have also changed with time; for instance, the sign for double *s* has become obsolete.

So we see that the changes in English speech have become very great over the centuries. Unfortunately, our spelling has not kept pace with the changes in our language and its pronunciation, with the result that English spelling causes confusion to ourselves as well as to foreigners.

Our *t* is sometimes *sh,* as in nation; sometimes soundless, as in listen; the *gh* may be an *f* in laugh, or not pronounced in night. The sound *k* was dropped in the beginning of such words as knight, knave, knock, but we keep to the same old spelling.

Many and various peoples have had a hand in the making of England, its language and pronunciation, its way of life and its alphabet. In essence, our alphabet is the Latin alphabet, which we have traced through the Greeks and Semites back to Egypt.

END

Many books have been written on the origin and history of writing. Most of them are now obsolete because of new archeological discoveries. Others are out of print and not easily available to the general reader. This short list of books is given for those who may be interested in extra reading.

Albright, W. F., *The Archaeology of Palestine,* Pelican Books, 1949.

Bloomfield, Leonard, *Language,* Holt, Reinhart & Winston, New York, 1933.

Ceram, C. W., *Gods, Graves and Scholars,* Alfred A. Knopf, Inc., New York, 1953.

Chadwick, John, *The Decipherment of Linear B,* Cambridge University Press, New York, 1958.

Chiera, Edward, *They Wrote on Clay,* University of Chicago Press, Chicago, 1938.

Clodd, Edward, *The History of the Alphabet,* New York, 1938.

Diringer, David, *The Alphabet,* Philosophical Library, Inc., New York, 1947.

Diringer, David, *Writing,* Thomas and Hudson, London, 1962.

Doblhofer, Ernst, *Voices in Stone,* Viking Press, New York, 1961.

Durant, Will, *Story of Civilization, (Our Oriental Heritage,* Vol. 1), Simon & Schuster, New York, 1954.

Gardiner, Sir Alan, *Egypt of the Pharaohs,* Oxford University Press, Oxford, 1961.

Gelb, I. J., *A Study of Writing,* University of Chicago, Chicago, 1963.

Irwin, Keith Gordon, *Man Learns to Write,* London, 1958.

Jeffery, Lilian H., *The Local Scripts of Archaic Greece"* Oxford University Press, Oxford, 1961.

Kühn, Herbert, *Rock Pictures of Europe,* Sidgwick and Jackson, London.

McMurtrie, Douglas C., *The Book,* Oxford University Press, 1943.

Mason, William A., *A History of the Art of Writing,* The Macmillan Co., New York, 1928.

Moorhouse, A. C., *The Triumph of the Alphabet,* Henry Schuman, New York, 1953.

Neugebauer, O., *The Exact Sciences in Antiquity,* Brown University Press, Providence, 1957.

Ogg, Oscar, *The 26 Letters,* Thomas Y. Crowell Co., New York, 1948.

Pedersen, Holger, *Linguistic Science in the 19th Century,* Harvard Press, 1931.

Pei, Mario, *The Story of Language,* J. B. Lippincott Co., New York, 1949.

Ullman, B. L., *Ancient Writing and Its Influence,* Longmans, Green and Co., New York, 1932.

169

ITALY
ADRIATIC SEA
Tarentes
Sybaris
Zancle
Croton
Corcyra
Syracuse
MŒSIA
Apollonia
BLACK
THRACE
Bosporus
Heraclea
Sinop
Therma
Byzantium
Cyzicus
BITHYNIA
Athos
Troy
Hatti
Olympus
GREECE
MYSIA
Pergamum
HITTITES
CAPPADOCIA
Delphi
Sardis
Thebes
Smyrna
LYDIA
Athens
Ephesus
Olympia
Mycene
Miletus
CARIA
Sparta
Pylos
Halycarnassus
CILICIA
Phaselis
Mallus
RHODES
Ugarit
Aptera
Knossos
Arvad
CYPRUS
Tripolis
CRETE
Byblus
Baritus
MEDITERRANEAN
Sidon
Tyre
Dar
SEA
PHOENICIA
PHILISTIA
Cyrene
Jeri
CYRENAICA
Rosetta
Pelusium
Gaza
EDOM
LYBIAN DESERT
Ezion G
Memphis
SINAI
Ammon
Mt Sinai
EGYPT
Akheaton
Arsinoe
Nile
RED
Temples
Thebes
SEA